One of the most difficult tasks in teaching theology to the church is to explain seemingly incomprehensible truths in a way that is clear, accurate, and understandable. The doctrine of the Trinity is one of those seemingly incomprehensible truths. However, I have not read a more accessible and well-written treatment than Donald Macleod's book, *Shared Life*. It is a truly enjoyable read and I am very thankful to see it republished in this new 30th anniversary edition. May the Lord use this excellent resource for a new generation. I commend it warmly.

NATE PICKOWICZ,
Pastor, Harvest Bible Church, Gilmanton Iron Works, New Hampshire; author, *Christ & Creed*

Shared Life offers readers the chance to sit once more in the classroom of one of the great Scottish theologians of the last century. Here we have Donald Macleod at his finest, constantly reminding us that the doctrine of the Trinity is far more than a topic for academic study. It is a truth with the potential to transform us as we draw near to consider the shared love of the Father, the Son, and the Holy Spirit.

HUNTER NICHOLSON,
Donald Macleod Researcher

The Christian doctrine of the Holy Trinity, when rightly appreciated, is one of the most precious truths on which a believer may meditate. For when we reverently contemplate the Trinity, we are at once pondering the deepest mystery of the faith and glorying in the nature of our transcendent God as he has revealed himself in the Scriptures. Nevertheless, this great doctrine has been neglected, misunderstood, and even attacked. It is apparent then that we all need to know more about this great biblical truth, and this book is a good starting place. For the beginner, *Shared Life* provides the ideal introduction. It is simple, clear, straightforward, and practical (without being superficial). *Shared Life* furnishes the reader with: a brief overview of biblical teaching on the Trinity; a quick summary of the historical development of the church doctrine of the Trinity; challenging practical application of this great truth to daily Christian living; and a helpful response to current attacks on the Christian doctrine of the Trinity. All of this, Macleod manages to squeeze into just over one hundred pages.

LIGON DUNCAN,
Chancellor, Reformed Theological Seminary,
Jackson, Mississippi

THE TRINITY AND THE
FELLOWSHIP OF GOD'S PEOPLE

30th
ANNIVERSARY EDITION

Shared Life

Donald Macleod

CHRISTIAN
FOCUS

Copyright © Donald Macleod

Hardback ISBN: 978-1-5271-1069-4
Ebook ISBN: 978-1-5271-1121-9

10 9 8 7 6 5 4 3 2 1

First published in 1994
Reprinted in 1999, 2002, 2005 and 2006

This 30th anniversary edition published in 2024
by
Christian Focus Publications Ltd,
Geanies House, Fearn, Ross-shire,
IV20 1TW, Great Britain

www.christianfocus.com

Designed and typeset by Pete Barnsley (CreativeHoot.com)

Printed by Gutenberg, Malta

Contents

Part 3 – Under Attack

PART 1

One God: Three Persons

Evidence from the Bible

The term *Trinity* does not occur in the Bible nor is there any single verse which sets out the doctrine in the precise words used by Christians down the ages. What we do have, however, is some very clear teaching involving three great facts: first, God is one; secondly, the Father, the Son and the Holy Spirit are God; and, thirdly, the Father, the Son and the Holy Spirit are distinct persons. The doctrine of the Trinity is an attempt to do justice to all of these points. To understand why the church expressed it in the terms familiar to us today we must look both at the biblical teaching and at the discussions which went on among Christians, particularly in the fourth century.

The doctrine itself is of vital importance to Christians. It is the one belief held in common by the people of God everywhere. It is crucial to our understanding of both God and man. And it is the model for the way we should live, particularly in our relations with one another. Only a proper understanding of it can produce a sense of mystery, the devotion of God and the true humanism which are the essence of religion.

The Old Testament

God is one

The single most important doctrine of the Old Testament is the unity of God: 'Hear, O Israel: The Lord our God, the Lord is one' (Deut. 6:4). This contrasted vividly with the beliefs of Israel's neighbours, most of whom were *polytheists*, believing that there were many gods. In effect this meant that each natural force (for example, the sun, the rain, the thunder, the fields, the seas) had its own god. The only advance on this was what is known as *henotheism*. Those who held this view believed that each land had its own god: other gods might be supreme in other lands, but their particular god was supreme in theirs.

Israel's faith was in stark contrast to all this. They believed that the Lord was exclusively God: he was God over the whole earth, the only God who actually lived and existed (Isa. 45:22). Other gods were idols but the Lord actually did things: he made the heavens (Ps. 96:5).

God's unity did not only mean that he was *the only God*, however. It also meant that he was *a single being*.

The Lord was one, possessing in himself every power and perfection of deity. He was the single source of grace, the single author of creation and the single object of worship.

The doctrine of the Trinity is not in any way a retreat from this Old Testament teaching. We may even say that Deuteronomy 6:4 is the most important text in the Bible for Christian faith. The unity of God is the bed-rock of our confession. When we confess Christ as Lord wc do not see him as a second God, but as identical with the Creator-Lord of the Old Testament.

God is more than one
But if the Old Testament is emphatic about the unity of God, it appears to have little to say about the second aspect of the doctrine of the Trinity, namely, the idea of more-than-oneness in God. The reason is simple. The writers of the Old Testament had to bend all their efforts to keep the people from idolatry and polytheism. Only when belief in the Lord as the one, exclusive deity was firmly established would it be appropriate to complicate matters by revealing that in the oneness of God there were the Father, the Son and the Holy Spirit. There is scarcely a hint of this in the Old Testament. In fact, no group possessing only the Old Testament has ever come to a knowledge of the doctrine of the Trinity.

Yet once we know that God is triune we can see some hints of it in the Old Testament. Augustine, in a famous saying, declared that what is patent in the New Testament is latent in the Old. More elaborately, he compared the Old

Testament to a room which is fully furnished but unlit. Until we have light, we cannot see what is there. Once we have light, everything is clear. Yet there is nothing there that wasn't there before.

Augustine's observations are particularly appropriate to the doctrine of the Trinity. Without the light of the New Testament we can see no hint of more-than-oneness in God. But once the New Testament reveals that God is represented by the Three, the Father, the Son and the Holy Spirit, we can see things in the Old Testament that point in the same direction. It is not the New Testament that puts these things there. It merely shows that they are there.

Elohim

One of these Old Testament hints is that the name most often used for God is *Elohim*. This word is plural in form. Grammatically, it should be translated *gods*. In fact, sometimes it refers to angels and then it is translated in the plural (compare Ps. 8:5 with Heb. 2:7). The important thing is that when it is used of the God of Israel it has a singular verb or adjective (as if we were to say, 'The gods *is*'). It would be too much to say that this very peculiar grammar *teaches* the doctrine of the Trinity. But it certainly agrees with it, and if we bear in mind that in the last analysis it was God who chose the language of the Old Testament (2 Tim. 3:16), we can now see that he had good reason for calling himself *Elohim*. The plural not only points to the truth that in him there is a concentration of *God-ness* but also fits in beautifully with the fact that in him there is a fulness of fellowship. The New Testament disclosure of the Father, the Son and the Holy Spirit is the best, and possibly the only, explanation of God's giving himself a plural name.

'Us' and 'our'

There is another hint of the doctrine of the Trinity in Genesis 1:26: 'Let *us* make man in *our* image, in *our* likeness'. These words can hardly refer, as some allege, to a consultation between God and the angels. Man was not made by the angels. Neither was he made in the image of the angels. God made man in his own image and the words of Genesis 1:26 indicate some consultation within God himself. We find similar language in Isaiah 6:8: 'Whom shall I send? And who will go for us?'

Neither of these passages is sufficient by itself to lead men to the belief that God is triune. But when we learn that doctrine from other sources (the New Testament), we can see at once that from the very beginning God was speaking in a way that expressed the deepest truths about himself, even though these truths could not yet be grasped by those to whom he was talking.

The Angel of the Lord

But the clearest of all hints of the Trinity in the Old Testament is the personage known as 'the Angel of the Lord'. The remarkable thing about him is that he is both distinguished from the Lord and identified with the Lord.

He is *distinguished* from the Lord, for example, in the very form of his name: the Angel *of* the Lord. He also speaks of God as someone distinct from himself. For example, in Genesis 16:11 the Angel says to Hagar, 'The LORD has heard of your misery'. Similarly, in Genesis 22:12 he says to Abraham, 'Now I know that you fear God'.

The distinction is even more emphatic in Genesis 24:40 in the words of Abraham to the servant he was sending to seek a wife for Isaac: 'The LORD... will send his angel with you and make your journey a success'.

Yet in other passages the Angel is clearly *identified* with God. One of the clearest instances of this is in Genesis 31:11-13: 'The angel of God said to me in the dream, "Jacob". I answered, "Here I am". And he said... "I am the God of Bethel... Now leave this land at once and go back to your native land"'. We find the same thing earlier in Genesis 16:10, in the Angel's words to Hagar, 'I will so increase your descendants that they will be too numerous to count': the Angel is promising to do something that lies only within the capability of God. He makes a similar promise to Abraham in Genesis 22:17: 'I will surely bless you and make your descendants as numerous as the stars in the sky and as the sand on the seashore'. In Genesis 48:16, the aged Jacob invokes the Angel of the Lord when blessing the sons of Joseph: 'The Angel who has delivered me from all harm – may he bless these boys'. Centuries later the prophet Hosea referred to another incident in the patriarch's life and wrote: 'As a man he struggled with God. He struggled with the angel and overcame him; he wept and begged for his favour. He found him at Bethel and talked with him there – the LORD God Almighty, the LORD is his name of renown!' (Hosea 12:3-5).

The Angel of the Lord was certainly not sent to reveal the doctrine of the Trinity. The great concern of the Old Testament, as we have seen, was to fix on the mind of Israel the fact that God is one. Any premature emphasis on the more-than-oneness would have increased the risk (grave enough already) of polytheism. The Angel came to *help* the people of God. He was the Lord's executive. Revelation of the innermost nature of God was not his mission. Yet, in the course of helping his people, he did incidentally disclose truth about God himself. Looking back at his work from the viewpoint of the New Testament we can now see that one can be sent from God and at the same time be himself God.

The New Testament

Before looking in detail at the New Testament teaching let us first notice a few general points.

The Trinity is revealed in salvation

First of all, the New Testament disclosure of the Trinity is closely related to the experience of salvation. The three-foldness in God is revealed not directly but in the course of redemption. The Father, the Son and the Holy Spirit each make a distinct contribution to our salvation and, as so often, God reveals what he is through what he does. Here, too, is another reason why the doctrine of the Trinity could not be revealed in the Old Testament. The full and final truth about God could become clear only in the completion of the work of salvation. Knowledge of the Trinity was simply impossible before Bethlehem and Pentecost.

The Trinity is presupposed

It is also worth noting that in the New Testament the doctrine of the Trinity is not something put forward aggressively. It is in the background as something presupposed, almost in the same way as we today assume that the earth is round and don't feel any need to keep reminding people of it.

The New Testament writers do not, for example, dogmatically state that Christ is God and then go on to defend and expound their position. Nor do they lay down aggressively their belief that the Holy Spirit is a person. When we open the New Testament we find the early Christians already in comfortable possession of these truths. We do not see these convictions growing, or attacked and defended, as we do, for example, the doctrine of justification by faith. In the very earliest books of the New Testament, Christians are already worshipping Jesus and calling him Lord.

Yet the writers are curiously lacking in any feeling of embarrassment over the matter. They certainly betray no sense of being innovators or revolutionaries. This is quite remarkable. All of them were Jews, with a firm, almost fanatical, belief in one God. Yet there they are worshipping

Jesus and the Holy Spirit as well as God the Father, while at the same time warning their readers against idolatry! The only possible explanation for this is that their belief in the Trinity is set firmly within the framework of their belief in one God. If the Son is Lord, he is the Lord of the Old Testament. If the Holy Spirit is Lord, he, too, is the Lord of the Old Testament. The appearance of the Son and of the Spirit does not work a sudden addition to the number of gods, but a revelation of previously unknown fulness and depth in the being of the one God himself.

Terms used

We must also notice, however, that the New Testament writers expressed these truths without the very specialised jargon which theologians use today. It was only after the New Testament books and letters had been written that, in the course of debate and controversy, the church introduced new words into the Christian religion: words like Trinity, person, essence, nature and substance. These words do not occur in the New Testament; at least not with the special meanings they bear today. This has created a difficulty for some Christians, who feel that we should not use non-biblical terms to express our beliefs. In fact, this was already a difficulty in John Calvin's day (1509-1564) and he met it head-on in an interesting paragraph of his famous *Institutes* (I.xiii,3). The objections were particularly strong against the use of the word *Person* and Calvin made three points in reply.

First, he agreed with the objectors to the extent of insisting that we are bound to speak of God as reverently as we are bound to think of him. This means that any non-biblical terms in our theology must be reverent, they must be used sparingly and modestly and they must be kept in subordination to the Scriptures.

Secondly, Calvin argued that if we were to proceed as the objectors wanted, all interpretation of Scripture would be impossible. We could do nothing but repeat the words of the Bible, being forbidden to express its meaning in our own terms.

Thirdly, he claimed that the terms objected to did no more than explain what the Scriptures declared and sanctioned, namely, that there are three who are called *god* and yet there is only one God. This, says Calvin, is 'dark and intricate' and we have every right to explain it in clearer terms.

The unity of God is re-emphasised

There is one other general point to be borne in mind. The New Testament deliberately emphasises the unity of God. It was not simply a part of the Old Testament teaching to be left behind once fuller light came. Nor was it something that lay only in the background. It was taught clearly and frequently. In 1 Corinthians 8:4, for example, Paul declares, 'We know that an idol is nothing at all in the world and that there is no God but one'. He writes similarly in Ephesians 4:4, 6: 'There is... one God and Father of all, who is over all and through all and in all'. James is equally explicit, if slightly ironic: 'You believe that there is one God. Good!' (James 2:19). There are many other similar passages (see Gal. 3:20; 1 Tim. 1:17; 1 Tim. 2:5; Jude 25). They make it absolutely clear that Christianity remains firmly committed to belief in one exclusive deity.

Matthew, Mark and Luke

Bearing these points in mind, let us go on to look at some New Testament passages which are Trinitarian in the sense of bringing all three persons, the Father, the Son and the Holy Spirit, before us simultaneously.

We see this very clearly, for example, in the story of the baptism of Jesus (Mark 1:9-11). The Father's voice comes from heaven, Jesus is acknowledged as the Son of God and the Holy Spirit descends upon him in the form of a dove. The Father, the Son and the Spirit are clearly not names for the same person. They act on one another, refer to one another and even serve one another. It is equally clear that each is divine. The Spirit comes from heaven. Jesus is the divine Son.

The allusion to the Three is even clearer in Matthew 28:19: 'Therefore go and make disciples of all nations, baptising them in the name of the Father and of the Son and of the Holy Spirit'. It is remarkable that such a profound theological point should occur at the heart of a great practical passage. Here, the Lord is giving the disciples their marching orders. They are to *go*. But their going is to be in order to teach (literally, to make disciples).

Furthermore, the teaching is to lead to conversion, confession and baptism. It is not, however, the simple name of Christ that the new believers are to confess and be baptised into. It is something much more complex: the name of the Father and of the Son and of the Holy Spirit. (We will explore the practical implications of this further on. If disciples are to be baptised into what they know and believe, then the preaching which makes them Christians must introduce them to all three persons of the Trinity. What does this mean for evangelism today?).

The actual wording of the Lord's statement here is very interesting. For example, he speaks of the name, not the names. It is one name: a reminder, again, of the unity of God. Yet that *one* name is now, 'The Father, the Son and the Holy Spirit'. It was passages such as this which led the early church to speak of three distinct 'persons'. This is particularly important with regard to the Holy Spirit, because we sometimes tend to think of him as only an abstract power or influence. If he were, he would hardly be mentioned in the same breath as the Father and the Son, whose 'personalness' no one disputes.

It probably would not have occurred to the early Christians (as it did to some later heretics) that these three were one and the same person. Events like the baptism of Christ and the day of Pentecost made the distinctions between the Father, the Son and the Spirit very clear. In fact, the Lord's own language in Matthew 28:19 distinguishes between them very carefully. He does not say, 'In the name of the Father, Son and Holy Spirit' but

'In the name of *the* Father and of *the* Son and of *the* Holy Spirit'. If all were covered by the one *the* then grammarians would tell us at once that Father, Son and Spirit must be one indivisible person. But the Lord repeats *the* before each title to safeguard the truth that although they share the one name they are distinct persons (something we already know from such facts as that the Father *sent* the Son and that the Holy Spirit *led* him).

The writings of John: John's Gospel

John's Gospel contains many of the profoundest words ever written by man and many of his most profound statements, in turn, refer to relations between the Father, the Son and the Holy Spirit. More than any other Christian writing, this Gospel impelled the church to work out what we know today as the doctrine of the Trinity. Yet we must bear in mind that John was not an academic writing for scholars and theologians. He was an apostle ministering to ordinary Christians. He expects them to try to understand his teaching and he expects such understanding to be good for their spiritual lives: 'This is eternal life: that they may know you, the only true God, and Jesus Christ, whom you have sent' (John 17:3).

Jesus: 'was God'

John launches out into the deep in the very opening words of his Gospel: 'In the beginning was the Word, and the Word was with God, and the Word was God' (John 1:1). 'The Word' refers, of course, to Jesus, the One who became flesh, lived among us and was pointed out by John the Baptist as 'the Lamb of God, who takes away the sin of the world' (John 1:14, 29). In the beginning, when God created the world, he did not create Jesus. Jesus (the Word) was already in being. In fact, he never came into being. He simply *was*. In theological jargon, the Word was a pre-existent, uncreated Being. It is not surprising, then, that John goes on to add, 'the Word was God'.

Jehovah's Witnesses like to point out that in this statement as we have it in the original Greek there is no definite article (*the*) before *God*. Therefore, they argue, John was not saying that Jesus was *God* but only that he was *a god*. But this is bad grammar and even worse theology.

There are very good reasons in the Greek idiom for omitting the definite article; and if Jesus is *a god*, who are the other gods? Is it conceivable that John, schooled in the Jewish belief that there is one God, should suddenly spring on us the idea that in fact there is a whole collection of deities? In fact, if the apostle wanted to say that the Word was God in the highest possible sense, then he chose the best possible form of words for saying so. The expanded translation of the New English Bible is very helpful at this point: 'what God was, the Word was'. As the church would later say in its great creeds, the Son is divine in exactly the same sense as the Father is divine.

Jesus: 'with God'

But John does not leave it there (and don't forget: he is writing for ordinary Christians). He adds that 'the Word was *with* God'. In this particular statement, God means *God the Father*. If we take this with the earlier assertion that the Word was God we end up with the remarkable idea of 'God with God'. This again highlights the distinction between the persons of the Trinity. The Word could not be the One that he himself was *with*. And even when he says *with*, John puts it in a most unusual way. Instead of using the ordinary word for *with*, he chooses a word which usually means *toward*: the Word was *toward* the Father. They lived towards each other. They *were* for each other. They reached out to each other, living, face to face, an existence of total love and total sharing.

Apart from all else, this gives added poignancy to what Jesus suffered on the cross. There, forsaken by God, he came to be without God. It would have been a dreadful experience for anyone. For Jesus, it was particularly awesome and traumatic because his whole existence had been so close to God. Throughout eternity there had been unbroken fellowship; and from Bethlehem to Calvary the Father had always been with him. Then, suddenly, and when most needed, he was not there. Instead of light, darkness; instead of an answer, silence; instead of reassurance, nothing.

Jesus in relation to the Father

The words of John 3:16 are often regarded as setting forth 'the simple gospel'. They do, of course, express the glory of the Father's love most memorably. But lucidity and simplicity are not the same thing. There is nothing simple about this utterance. Indeed, we cannot make any sense of it without the doctrine of the Trinity. It is not a statement about Jesus, but about the Father: *he* gave his only Son. The whole glory of the action lies in the special relationship between Jesus and the Father. He is God's Son; and he is God's Son at the moment when he is given (not, as some have taught, only after the resurrection).

Furthermore, he is the Son in a totally unique sense: the only-begotten, the only such Son that God has. This is the way the New Testament usually speaks when commenting, with wonder, on what God the Father did at Calvary. In Romans 8:32, for example, we are told that God did not spare *his own* Son. Earlier in the same chapter Paul speaks of God *sending* his own Son (Rom. 8:3). The point being made all the time is that we can never understand the cross unless we remember, first, that it was the Father's act and, secondly, that Jesus was very, very special to the Father. He was, as Colossians 1:13 indicates, 'the Son he loves' (literally, 'the Son of his love').

The way the New Testament puts this often reminds us of the story of Abraham offering up Isaac (Gen. 22). The words of verse 2 are especially poignant: 'Take your son, your only son Isaac, whom you love, and go to the region of Moriah. Sacrifice him there as a burnt offering'. Isaac was uniquely precious to Abraham, but certainly not more so than the eternal Son was to the eternal Father. It is not difficult to imagine the cost to Abraham of sacrificing his son. But that cost depended entirely on the special and unique relationship between them. In the same way the magnificence of Calvary surely consists in the fact that God the Father did not shrink from the cost of the cross: a cost which derives entirely from the unique and eternal love between the Father and the Son. If the Father and the Son were one and the same person, we completely destroy John 3:16. Equally, if Jesus was a mere man or a mere creature we destroy John 3:16.

The relation of Father, Son and Spirit

There is an interesting cluster of statements about the Father, the Son and the Spirit in John chapter 14. In verse 16, Jesus says, 'I will ask the Father and he will give you another Counsellor'. These words clearly imply that Jesus is not the Father, nor is he the Holy Spirit. The three are distinct persons. This passage also indicates that the Holy Spirit is no mere power. He is not *the comfort* which God gives or *the help* which God sends. He is the *Comforter* and the *Helper*.

Yet the connection between Jesus and the Spirit is a very close one. He is *another* Helper, distinct from Jesus, but in him Jesus himself comes: 'I will not leave you as orphans; I will come to you' (John 14:18).

There is an equally close relation between Jesus and the Father: 'I am in the Father and the Father is in me' (John 14:11). Each dwells in the other and this becomes the pattern for the way in which God dwells in his people (John 17:21).

This closeness between the Father and the Son is brought out even more fully in John 10:30, 'I and the

Father are one'. The same language is used, however, of the unity of the church in John 17:21. Again, we will be looking at the implications of this further on. This warns us against the idea that the Father merges himself in the Son, or *vice versa*. The unity of the church does not destroy the individuality of believers. Neither does the unity of the Father and the Son destroy the individuality of either.

John's letters

According to some versions, 1 John 5:7 reads as follows: 'There are three that bear witness in heaven, the Father, the Word and the Holy Spirit; and these three are one'. This is the most explicit Trinitarianism to be found in the Bible. It is rightly omitted, however, from most modern versions because, as the translators of the New International Version point out, our only authority for these words is a few late manuscripts of the Vulgate (a fourth-century Latin translation). *Late* in this case means the sixteenth century. It would be dishonest and foolish to use this passage to support our doctrine: a good case does not need bad arguments.

The writings of Paul

Paul's letters are the earliest of the New Testament writings (with the possible exception of James). The apostle's opening greetings are particularly interesting for the doctrine of the Trinity. They have a standard form: 'Grace and peace from God our Father and the Lord Jesus Christ'. The fascinating thing here is that the Father and

Jesus are presented as equally the source of 'grace and peace'. This would be utterly irreverent and incongruous if Jesus were only a creature, however eminent. He can be mentioned in the same breath as God the Father only because he is equal with God the Father (Phil. 2:6).

The greeting in Ephesians is unusual because Paul expands it. It occurs in its usual form in Ephesians 1:2: 'Grace and peace from God the Father and the Lord Jesus Christ'. But this is followed by a great passage in which Paul expresses his gratitude to the three persons of the Trinity (although he does not, of course, use this language): to God the Father, who has blessed us in Christ; to Christ, in whom we have redemption; and to the Holy Spirit, who is the pledge of our inheritance.

Sometimes the way Paul signs off his letters is equally interesting. The apostle's life is so bound up with his theology that it controls even the layout of his correspondence! The conclusion to Ephesians, for example, reads: 'Peace to the brothers, and love with faith from God the Father and the Lord Jesus Christ'. But the trinitarianism is even clearer in the benediction of 2 Corinthians. Here, Paul brings the three persons before us as, equally, the source of all that Christians have a right to hope for: 'May the grace of the Lord Jesus Christ, and the love of God, and the fellowship of the Holy Spirit be with you all'.

It is worth noting, too, that Paul does not regard the order 'Father/Son/Spirit' as sacrosanct. In 2 Corinthians 13:14, for example, the order is Son/

Father/Spirit. But even this is not strictly accurate. Paul does not use the language of the traditional doctrine of the Trinity. Instead of Father, *Son*, Spirit he speaks of Father, *Lord*, Spirit. At the very least, this should warn us against dogmatism and inflexibility in stating our own doctrine.

2

The First Christian Thinkers

By the end of the first century the last book of the New Testament had been written and the teaching of the apostles given permanent written form. Through that teaching (confirmed in their own experience) the early Christians found themselves in possession of a wide range of convictions, including the following:

- There is one God.

- Salvation comes from a threefold source: the Father, the Son and the Holy Spirit.

- Christ is God.

- The Holy Spirit, their loving, wise and powerful Helper, is a person.

- The Father is not the Son, nor is the Son the Holy Spirit.

None of these beliefs, taken by itself, was difficult to understand. But it was exceedingly difficult to work out how they could all be held together. How could God be one and three at the same time? In what sense was the Son *God?* What was the relation between the Son and the Father, and the Son and the Spirit? Soon these questions were agitating the church and dangerous answers were being offered by theological speculators. Some asserted that *Father, Son* and *Spirit* were only different names for the same person. Others taught that Jesus was not God's Son eternally but only became Son when *adopted* by God at the resurrection. Yet others cut the knot by denying, outrightly, that Christ was God in any real sense at all. He was only a creature.

Tertullian: laying the foundations

Providentially, God raised up a succession of theological giants to deal with these issues. The first of them was Tertullian, who lived and worked in North Africa between 160 and 220 A.D. Tertullian was a lawyer by profession, but he also had some learning in medicine and literature and probably some knowledge of military affairs as well. He was converted to Christ relatively late in life, but the wasted years were compensated for by the fact that 'he brought in his hands all the spoils of antique culture' (B.B. Warfield, *Studies in*

Tertullian and Augustine, Oxford University Press, New York, p 3.)

Tertullian had to deal with the problems created by a gentleman called Praxeas, of whom we know nothing except what we read in Tertullian's own pamphlet, *Against Praxeas*. He taught that the Son had no independent existence: the Father and the Son were one and the same being. If we are to believe Tertullian (and why not?) Praxeas put this very crudely. It was the Father himself who descended into the Virgin, became his own Son, and suffered and died (his heresy is sometimes called *Patripassianism* because it teaches that it was the Father who suffered). Tertullian was not inclined to mince his words either. He accused Praxeas of 'doing the Devil's work at Rome. He exiled the Paraclete' (a reference to Praxeas' assault on spiritual gifts) 'and crucified the Father'.

Praxeas, no doubt, was a puny adversary, but his teachings provoked Tertullian to think and to write and, in doing so, to lay the foundations of what we know today as the doctrine of the Trinity.

But what did Tertullian actually say?

First of all, he emphasised very firmly *the unity of God*. Their very rule of faith, he says, withdraws Christians from the world's plurality of gods: 'We believe that there is only one God'.

Secondly, he asserts that *the Father and the Son were distinct*: 'We believe that there is only one God, but that this one only God has also a Son, his Word, who proceeded from himself'. He quotes 1 Corinthians 15:24: 'Then the end will come, when he hands over the kingdom to God the Father after he has destroyed all dominion, authority and power'. 'From this one passage,' says Tertullian, 'we are able to show that the Father and the Son are two separate persons.'

Thirdly, he worked out *the terminology the church needed* to express its beliefs as clearly and precisely as possible. In fact, this was Tertullian's main achievement. To this day we are using the words which he introduced into theology.

For example, he spoke of the *Trinity*: 'The unity which derives the Trinity from its own self is so far from being destroyed that it is actually supported by it'. (What that sentence means doesn't matter! We are only interested in the word *Trinity*.) It is worth noting, too, that *Trinity* does not mean *threeness*. Tertullian makes it plain that what he means is *three in one*.

Tertullian also used the word *essence* or *being*, particularly to express the sense in which God is one. God's unity, he taught, was one of essence: 'These three are one in essence'. The Father, the Son and the Spirit are one Being.

But probably Tertullian's major innovation was to bring in the word *person*. He used this to distinguish between the way in which God is one and the way in which he is three. 'The three persons,' he writes, 'are of One, by unity of essence.' Again: 'These three are one in essence, not in person'. The word (which does not occur in the New Testament) found its way into the creeds and confessions of the church and, from there, into its theology, worship and devotion.

Yet the church was never entirely happy with it (and probably Tertullian was not altogether happy with it either). It was easily misunderstood. In Latin, it meant originally a mask, then an actor in a play; but the Father, the Son and the Spirit were not actors and they were certainly not masks. Later, the Latin word *persona* came to mean virtually *an individual*. A human person was a separate being from every other human person. Tertullian would certainly not have wanted the word *person* understood in this way. When he said that there were three persons in the Godhead he did not mean that there were three separate divine beings.

These misgivings found expression in a famous statement by Augustine: 'When the question is asked, "What three?" human language labours altogether under great poverty of speech. The answer, however, is given, Three "persons", not that it might be (completely) spoken, but that it might not be left (wholly) unspoken' (*On the Trinity*, Book V, Ch. 9).

The fact is, of course, that the whole truth about God cannot be spoken. While it is easy enough to see the difficulties with Tertullian's language, it is not so easy to improve on it: God was one Being, but three Persons; or, in the Being of the one God there were three Persons. In the world of Tertullian's day, the groups *thing, animal* or *person* would have corresponded roughly to today's *animal, vegetable* or *mineral*. The Father, the Son and the Spirit were obviously neither *things* nor *animals*, and *person* was the only category left. Furthermore, (bear in mind that Tertullian was a lawyer), a person was what you could take to court and accuse or defend and praise or blame (you could do none of these things with *things* or *animals*). Above all, a person was what had feelings and was capable of love and affection.

What better word could there be for the Father, the Son and the Spirit? They were not things or animals. They could be praised and thanked. They could be loved. Furthermore, not only did the one God love the world but each Person within the Trinity loved the others. The Son, for example, was the Father's 'only beloved'.

While it is important, therefore, to remember the limitations of the word *person* we have not so far been able to think of a better. Tertullian's word has proved very serviceable and we should be thankful to him for suggesting it.

Athanasius: the deity of Christ

The second theological giant associated with the doctrine of the Trinity was Athanasius. As a young deacon he was present at the Council of Nicea (325 A.D.). In 328 he was appointed Bishop of Alexandria. Like Tertullian, he had had a liberal education. He was also an expert biblical scholar and a man of profound religious temperament (he was one of the founders of the monastic movement). Athanasius is one of the great, heroic figures of the Christian church, who for many years stood almost alone against the world, contending for the deity of Christ and suffering persecution and exile for his pains. These early theologians were no closet saints.

Arius

But we cannot understand Athanasius without mentioning another man: Arius. Arius was a presbyter (priest) in Alexandria who, around 318 A.D., began to agitate the church with his denial of the deity of Christ. The Son of God, he contended, was not eternal. He had a beginning, by being created. Arius put this in a famous epigram: 'There was when he was not'. Such flagrant heresy would probably not have caused the church much bother. But things are seldom that simple. Arius sugared the pill by saying that although the Son was a creature, he was not an *ordinary* creature. He was a kind of middle being, neither God nor man (nor angel), but somewhere in between God and the highest kind of creature.

The Council of Nicea

In 325 bishops from every part of the church gathered at Nicea (the modern town of Iznik on the western coast of Turkey, between the Dardanelles and the Black Sea) to deal with the Arian heresy. Three different parties were represented: the Arian, the Orthodox and (as always) a group who sat on the fence and are usually called Semi-Arians. The Orthodox were led by Alexander, Bishop of Alexandria, ably assisted by Athanasius (who could not be a member of the Council since he was not yet a bishop).

It was they who drafted what eventually became the official communiqué of the Council: the Nicene Creed. (This is not to be confused with 'the Nicene Creed' which is used in the Anglican Church and printed at the back of many hymnaries. This latter creed should really be called 'the Niceano-Constantinopolitan Creed' – we will refer to its origins later.) This was drafted expressly to exclude Arianism from the church by inserting a statement with which no Arian could possibly agree, namely, that the Son was one and the same in nature (*homoousios*) with God the Father. This emphatically ruled out the idea that he was a creature or some kind of in-between being. He shared in the very *being* of God himself. He had the same nature, the same status and the same prerogatives.

But those who thought the Council would bring peace were mistaken. It was only a signal for violent renewal of the struggle. Arius continued his agitation, stirring up opposition to the Nicene Creed and engaging in a campaign of propaganda and intrigue. The Semi-Arian party, in particular, grew in strength, opposing the Nicene slogan, *homoousios*, with their own slogan *homoiousios*, a word which meant that the Son was *like* God. He was similar in essence. This was a natural position for moderates to take. It was true and it would make peace and diplomats of all shades could agree to it. But Athanasius refused to be conned. Whatever was only *like* God was infinitely removed from *being* God. He continued the battle and the controversy raged over the whole of the East. Centuries later, Gibbon, author of

The Decline and Fall of the Roman Empire, made the gibe that the world was at war over an iota (HOMOOUSIOS v HOMO*I*OUSIOS). But the remark was more witty than perceptive. After all, there is only one letter of a difference between *theist* and *atheist*; and there is not all that much difference between *creator* and *creature*.

In fact, when we look at the teaching of Athanasius, its most striking feature is that he was driven by an overriding religious concern. The very heart of Christianity, as he saw it, was that Christ was *worshipped*, and the church's concept of him must agree with her practice. Arianism would be idolatry: the worship of a creature. 'Who ever thought,' exclaims Athanasius, 'that having abolished the worship of creatures we are to return to it again!' Elsewhere he writes: 'If our Saviour is neither God nor the Word nor the Son then let the Arians no longer be ashamed to think and talk as pagans and Jews do.'

It was not only a matter of the sinfulness of worshipping a creature, however. A Christ who was less than divine could never be a real *Saviour*. If he himself were not truly the Son of God, how could we become sons of God through him? 'There cannot be adoption apart from the real Son.'

These, and not academic ambition or the love of controversy, were the concerns that drove Athanasius. On a personal level, his principles cost him dearly, but by his persistence and insight, eloquence, courage and scholarship, the church came into secure possession of the truths which have sustained her faith ever since: Christ is the eternal Son of God; he possesses everything that constitutes God-ness; and we are to offer to him exactly the same worship as we offer to God the Father.

Later fine-tuning

Nicea, however, was a long time ago. Have there been no developments since? There have, but they have consisted largely in applying fine-tuning to the work of Tertullian and Athanasius.

The Creed of Constantinople

First, in the years after Athanasius more attention was paid to the Holy Spirit. In the original Nicene Creed he received scarcely a mention. All that was said was, 'We believe in the Holy Spirit'. In 381, however, there was a second Ecumenical Council, held this time at Constantinople. This Council, too, produced a creed, which, as I said already, ought to be called the Niceano-Constantinopolitan Creed but which (to confuse ordinary mortals!) is often called 'the Nicene Creed'.

The important thing about this Creed is that it had much more to say about the Holy Spirit, describing him as 'the Lord and Life-giver, proceeding from the Father, and with the Father and the Son to be worshipped and glorified'. In effect, this was applying the idea of *homoousios* to the Holy Spirit. He, as well as the Son, had the same nature as God the Father. The theologians mainly responsible for this development are usually referred to as 'the great Cappadocians' (because they came from a district of that name in what is now Turkey): Basil the Great, his brother,

Gregory Nyssa, and their friend, Gregory of Nazianzen. The last-named, in particular, stressed that the great word which Nicea had applied to the Son must also be applied to the Holy Spirit: 'What, then? Is the Spirit God? Most certainly. Well then, is he consubstantial (*homoousios*)? Yes, if he is God' (*The Fifth Theological Oration*, X).

John of Damascus

Another man who made an important contribution was John of Damascus (700-754). What he clarified was the way we are to distinguish the persons from each other. We know that each performs his own special work in creation and redemption. But, before there was any creation, and supposing there had to be no redemption, how did they differ *in themselves*? John's conclusion was that the Father, the Son and the Holy Spirit each has, to our view, one distinguishing personal property: the Father begets, the Son is begotten, and the Holy Spirit proceeds. 'In these three personal properties alone,' wrote John, 'do the three holy persons differ from each other' (*Exposition of the Orthodox Faith*, Chapter VIII). We should note the word *alone*. In everything but the *personal properties* (in nature, authority and in glory) the Father, the Son and the Holy Spirit are one.

The Council of Toledo

But the most dramatic development came in another area. The Creed of 381 declared that the Holy Spirit proceeded from the Father. Did he also proceed from the Son?

Theologians in the West, especially the great Augustine, began to say that he did, speaking of a *double procession* of the Spirit, that is, from the Father *and from the Son*. This idea found official recognition for the first time at the Synod of Toledo, in 589, but this was only a local council and did not carry much weight. After it, however, versions of the Creed containing the fateful phrase *and from the Son* began to circulate in the Western (Latin-speaking) church, especially in Spain and France.

For a long time the Popes refused to sanction the change in wording, but in 1044 Pope Benedict VIII finally gave it his approval and the word *filioque* (the Latin for *and from the Son*) became part of the official text of the Creed as used in the Western church. The Eastern church never accepted the change. In fact it took great umbrage and in 1054 it severed communion with the West. Officially, at least, the rift continues to the present day.

We must note very carefully that this dispute over the *filioque* clause is not about the Spirit, but about the Son. It is really the old question of the *homoousios* in another form. If the Son is in all respects equal to the Father then he must be equal to him in his relation to the Holy Spirit. Otherwise, the Son is inferior.

John Calvin

Which brings us to the last major contribution to the doctrine of the Trinity, that of John Calvin. The debate about the Spirit proceeding from the Son as well as from the Father highlighted a problem which had been present from the very beginning. Even the giants, Tertullian and Athanasius, had sometimes spoken of the Son in a way which suggested that he was inferior and subordinate to the Father. They sometimes described him as *derived* and as only a portion of the whole Godhead. They spoke of the Father as the First Principle of the Godhead, as its Fountain and Beginning, *communicating* being to the Son.

John Calvin was unhappy with all this. When people said that the Father alone was God in his own right, he protested that such teaching contradicted every Scripture which made Christ *God*. Deity could not be subordinate, neither could it owe its existence to someone else (after all, what was more characteristic of deity than self-existence?). Christ, if he were God, could not owe his being to any superior divinity. He must be God 'from his very self'. In respect of eternity, status and independence he must be fully the Father's equal.

In Calvin, the essential teaching of Tertullian, Athanasius and the Nicene fathers at last came fully into its own. The Son and the Holy Spirit are one and the same in nature with God the Father. Each Person, therefore, is God in his own right.

Bringing it all together

What firm conclusions, then, has the church reached through the many centuries of meditation and debate?

First, God is one. For Christians, no less than for Jews and Muslims, Deuteronomy 6:4 is the most important text in the whole Bible: 'The LORD our God, the LORD is one'.

Secondly, this God who is one being and has one name has revealed himself as 'the Father, the Son and the Holy Spirit'. Each of these is a person in the sense that each is distinct from the other and each is capable of knowing, feeling and, above all, loving. This is particularly important with regard to the Holy Spirit. He is not an *it* but a *he*. He is not mere *power* but Christ's *helper*, upholding and leading him throughout his earthly ministry. He is also *our* helper. Far from being a cold and detached abstraction he *groans* for us (Rom. 8:26) and is frequently even *hurt* by us (Eph. 4:30).

Thirdly, each of the three persons is God in the fullest possible sense. They share the one being, the one name and the one government. Each possesses everything that makes God, God; and each is to be worshipped with exactly the same reverence, love and adoration.

Which already reminds us that the doctrine of the Trinity is not simply something to be believed, but something that ought to affect our lives profoundly. How? That is what we shall look at in the next chapter.

PART 2

Trinitarian Religion

3

Our Understanding of God

Knowing and doing the truth

As we have seen, the men to whom we owe the doctrine of the Trinity were not cloistered, dry-as-dust academics. Tertullian, Athanasius and Calvin were men of outstanding personal piety, actively involved in human affairs, deeply concerned for the church and quite willing to suffer for their beliefs. They taught and defended the doctrine of the Trinity because, at the deepest level, it mattered to them.

But why did it matter? And why should it matter to us?

The most obvious reason is 'because the doctrine is true'. Our twentieth-century minds want to rush on at once to ask, 'but what is it good for?' We tend to be interested only in what is useful and to be impatient with what is only true. Surely, however, truth is important for its own sake. Even if the Christian life could be reduced to an endless round of singing and praying (and, of course, it cannot) we have to sing and pray with the *understanding* (1 Cor. 14:15). Besides, God has gone to enormous trouble to teach us the truth and we should surely take some trouble to learn it. In fact, if we love God such learning will not be a trouble. It will be a joy. Two young people in love will often say to one another, 'Tell me more about yourself.' The same is true of any real relationship with God. The more we learn about him, the happier we are: 'This is eternal life: that they may know you, the only true God, and Jesus Christ, whom you have sent' (John 17:3).

Yet we cannot ignore the warning given long ago by Thomas à Kempis: 'Of what use is it to discourse learnedly on the Trinity, if you lack humility and therefore displease the Trinity? Lofty words do not make a man just or holy; but a good life makes him dear to God' (*The Imitation of Christ*, Penguin, 1952, p 27). God has not given us the great doctrines merely for our intellectual amusement. He has given them so that they will make a difference to the way we live. Biblical belief should lead to biblical practice.

Even here, however, we need to be careful. What do we mean by *practical* ? We think immediately of humanitarianism: of assisting our neighbours, of relieving famine in Africa, of ministering to drug addicts and alcoholics. *Practical* is seen almost exclusively in terms of this world. Such thinking looks harmless enough, but what it actually makes us say is this: loving our neighbour is practical, loving God is not. As Christians we obviously have no right to think like that. Practical Christianity will certainly involve concern for our fellow man and good-will towards our neighbour wherever we meet him. But it begins with loving God, and with expressing that love in humility, gratitude and obedience.

Understanding God

At the level of personal religion, then, the doctrine of the Trinity is important, first of all, for our whole attitude to God.

God is a mystery

For example, it reminds us that God is a mystery. It has been said (probably more than once) that if he were small enough to be understood he would not be great enough to be worshipped. It would certainly be fatal to any doctrine of God that it contained nothing inscrutable. In Christianity, the central mystery is that God is triune: one being in three persons. However we explain or illustrate such a statement we are soon out of our depth. We have no experience of such an existence. In fact, it seems to contradict all that we know from our own experience. With us 'three persons' means 'three separate individuals'. How can it be different for God?

We can, of course, offer some explanation, so that the doctrine is not absurd. God is not one *in the same sense* as he is three. He is one in being, three in persons. But that does not carry us far.

The truth is that the very first assumption we have to make when we set out to understand God is that we have little, finite minds and that there is no way that he can be made to fit neatly into our words and concepts. A point comes (soon) when we have to stop speaking and writing because words fail us. That is not a point, however, at which we have to give up believing, on the ground that the whole thing is absurd. It is not even a point where we have stopped understanding. We have understood that God cannot be fully understood. We have come to the point (arguably the highest point in religious experience) where we glimpse the abyss which revelation has opened up for us and cry with Paul: 'Oh, the depth of the riches of the wisdom and knowledge of God! How unsearchable his judgments, and his paths beyond tracing out!' (Rom. 11:33). 'A science without mystery is unknown,' wrote Henry Drummond: 'a religion without mystery is absurd.'

God in fellowship

Secondly, the doctrine of the Trinity helps us to understand what John meant when he wrote, 'God is love'. Suppose God were not triune. Suppose he had no Son and no Holy Spirit. Whom, then, did he love? How could he be love if there were none to love? We cannot say that he was love because his heart went out towards the world. The world is only of yesterday, God is eternal. Does that mean that until yesterday (when he created the world) God could not be love? Remember, too, the story of Adam and the animals in Genesis 2:19-23. God parades them all before him and Adam is able to name them. But not one of them is a suitable partner for the man. He needed the love of his own kind, which is why he is so thrilled when Eve appears: 'This is now bone of my bones and flesh of my flesh'. What was true of Adam was, surely, also true of God. He needed the love of his own kind.

Once we see that God is triune, everything is much clearer. The Father was never lonely. He never lacked someone to love because from the beginning he had the fellowship of the Son and the Spirit. God was never a solitary in the midst of a vast emptiness: in the beginning, the Word was with God. As we have seen, *with* here really means *towards*. The Father and the Son lived face-to-face, in a love which was gloriously dynamic and outgoing.

God's independence

Which already brings us to the third thing: the doctrine of the Trinity helps us to understand the independence of God. He did not need to create a world to give himself 'an interest'; or man, made in his image, to provide an outlet for his love. There was in him no need or defect which a creation could make good. The fellowship of Father, Son and Holy Spirit was already a sufficiency. Each had not only himself but the others. There was the fulness of God to love and the fulness of God to enjoy. Against such a background we have to see the decision to create as an act of sheer grace in which God chooses to extend the circle of being, fellowship and love beyond himself.

God's completeness

In the same way, the doctrine of the Trinity helps us to understand what the Bible calls the blessedness of God (1 Tim. 1:11). The general idea here is that God is happy. He is free from all tension, frustration, deprivation, discontent, anxiety: instead, there is peace, harmony and fulfilment. As things are now, God's blessedness derives to some extent from his creation. For example, his profound satisfaction with the work of the six days is registered in the fact that he pronounced it very good (Gen. 1:31), and rested. He expressed similar delight in the work of the Mediator: 'You are my Son, whom I love; with you I am well pleased' (Mark 1:11). And when he presents us to himself 'faultless', he does so with great joy (Jude 24). But the real, eternal foundation of God's blessedness lies in the threefoldness of the divine life. What is true of the Christian is true even more splendidly of God. If for us to live is Christ (Phil. 1:21), if he is all our desire (Ps. 73:25), if our hearts find rest in him (Matt. 11:28), how much more is this true of God the Father? If *we* enjoy 'fulness' in Christ (Col. 2:10), much more do the persons of the Trinity find fulness in *each other*.

4

Our Attitude to Human Beings

The doctrine of the Trinity is equally important for our attitude to man. In this connection the story of creation makes two important points.

A planned creation

First, before the creation of man there is a divine council: 'Let *us* make man in *our* image' (Gen. 1:26). Up to this point the story has run smoothly, without interruption, through the work of the various days. But now there is a pause. Not only is man dignified by being created last, his creation is preceded by deliberation. We cannot take this as a reference to some conference between God and the angels, if only because humans are not made in the image of angels. In the light of the total biblical portrait of God we must take it to mean a deliberation between the Father, the Son and the Holy Spirit.

This is a measure of the uniqueness and importance of humanity. Man is not the haphazard outcome of thoughtless and blind evolution, nor even the result of some infinitely remote decision, 'Let there be a universe, and let it include people'. He is the result of specific divine reflection and consultation. There are, of course, other points in the Genesis account which emphasise man's lowliness and remind him very firmly that he is a creature. For example, he is made of the dust (Gen. 2:7) and he is made on the same day as other animals (Gen. 1:24, 26). But this cannot take away from the fact that all the deliberative wisdom of God, Father, Son and Holy Spirit, goes into making mankind what it is: the apex of creation.

In the image of the Trinity

Secondly, the creation story highlights the fact that we are made in the image of God: 'Let us make man in our image, in our likeness' (Gen. 1:26). It is not merely *my* image. It is *our* image. The image we bear is that of the triune God and, true though it is that this image has been marred in the Fall, it has never been lost. It still remains.

Two passages in the Bible make this unmistakably clear. In Genesis 9:6, God says: 'Whoever sheds the blood of man, by man shall his blood be shed; for in the image of God has God made man.' The important thing here is that the words describe the way things are now. *Human life is sacred* because man retains, even after the flood, the image of God.

The second passage is James 3:9: 'With the tongue we praise our Lord and Father, and with it we curse men, who have been made in God's likeness.' James is reminding us how serious a sin it is to use our tongues to hurt and destroy other people and the reason for its being so serious is that human beings still bear the image of God.

What does this mean for us today?

Equality

It means, first of all, that all human beings are *of equal worth*. Each bears the image of God. This is true regardless of sex: 'So God created man in his own image, in the image of God he created him; male and female he created them' (Gen. 1:27).

It is also true regardless of race. The Jews or the Athenians or the Afrikaaners may feel superior but before God we are all equal: 'From one man [God] made every nation of men' (Acts 17:26). We have a common ancestry, regardless of pigment or culture. We bear God's image whether we are free or slaves, learned or unlearned, skilled or unskilled, employed or unemployed, successes or failures, tycoons or beggars, martinets or addicts. Wherever we see a human being, there we see the image of God.

Diversity

Secondly, the fact that we bear God's image puts a premium on *individuality*. As we have seen, each person in the Trinity has his own incommunicable characteristic: something which is true of him alone and distinguishes him from the others. Admittedly, the theologians were really struggling when they tried to say what this distinctive thing was and managed only to say that the Father begets, the Son is begotten and the Holy Spirit proceeds. But however difficult it is to define, the fact itself is clear enough. The Father differs from the Son and both are different from the Holy Spirit.

This is clearly reflected in mankind. While we share a common humanity, each of us is a unique individual. We are unique genetically. We are unique in temperament. We are unique in gifts. God made us such. God loves us as such. He sympathises with us as such. He expects service from us as such. And he expects us to accept ourselves as such. There are times, inevitably, when, like Job, we despise ourselves (Job 42:6); or, as Woody Allen is supposed to have put it, 'My one regret in life is that I am not somebody else'. But wholesome repentance is one thing. Self-disparagement and self-rejection are another. We have the self that God gave us and which he has accepted 'in the Beloved'. To that self he says, '*You* are the salt of the earth... *you* are the light of the world' (Matt. 5:13, 14).

Community

Thirdly, the fact that we bear the divine image means that we are *made for fellowship*. This is probably the most important point of all. As bearers of God's image, we are made for 'withness'. As God himself observed, 'It is not good for the man to be alone' (Gen 2:18). There is a social life in the Godhead itself. The Father, the Son and the Holy Spirit live in community and fellowship. The same must be true of us. It is something we see exemplified beautifully in the life of Christ himself. He surrounded himself with people, both male and female. He related spontaneously and easily to children (Mark 10:14). He chose twelve simply 'to be with him' (Mark 3:14). He had an inner circle of three specially close friends (Peter, James and John), a home where he felt particularly welcome and secure (the home of Mary, Martha and Lazarus at Bethany) and one disciple (John, 'the disciple whom Jesus loved') with whom he had a particularly close bond.

Independence or commitment?

All this is in marked contrast to many of the trends we see around us today, when so many people try to find fulfilment in 'independence', as if they could be themselves only by escaping from relationships. We see this in the young people who leave home to seek the anonymity of a city bed-sit. We see it, too, in the lovers who refuse the commitment of marriage. In fact, our generation often gives the impression that we are terrified of giving ourselves to one another. Relationships are casual and open-ended, with clear escape routes.

This is clearly at variance with the fact that we bear the image of God. We are made to live face-to-face with others of our own kind.

This is clearly reflected, for example, in the divine institution of marriage, which is based, quite deliberately, on the fact already noticed that it is not good for individuals to be alone. Marriage presupposes, of course, that the partners are different.

One is male and one is female and, added to that, there are other differences of temperament, intelligence, background and experience. There may also be differences of race, colour and language. Yet in marriage these differences are transcended, as the two lives come together to form 'one flesh'. There is an inevitable loss of 'independence' as property, income, joys, sorrows, friends, relations, ambitions and decisions are shared.

But this loss of 'independence' is not an impoverishment. It is an enrichment as we enter upon a life of mutual love and service. The wife becomes a helper to her husband (Gen. 2:18). He nourishes and cherishes her (Eph. 5:29). And in Christian marriage, each enjoys the security of knowing that nothing but death will separate them. It is a commitment 'for better, for worse, for richer, for poorer', without escape routes. It is exclusive. And it is for ever.

All this is within the Trinitarian pattern. The three persons of the Godhead share a common being, dominion and purpose. They have exclusive relationships (Jesus is the only-begotten). And they have irreversible commitments.

The principle of a shared life also finds expression in the family, where we live with our fathers and mothers, brothers and sisters. We may also have an extended family, involving grandparents, cousins, aunts and uncles. Here again existence is face-to-face; and here, too, the foundation is love. In fact, the New Testament even has special words for it: *storge* for family affection and *philadelphia* for brotherly love. Families have shared privileges, experiences, resources, commitments and problems.

Of course, the Bible envisages that one day we shall leave this unit: 'For this reason a man will leave his father and mother and be united to his wife, and they will become one flesh' (Gen. 2:24). But we must note the setting. The passage does not envisage our choosing to 'leave the nest' in order to go off on our own to live in solitude. We leave to marry. In fact, it is very doubtful whether there is ever a time in life (for example, adolescence) when it is good for a person to be alone.

The same principle lies behind the impetus to friendship. It expresses something basic to our nature and was exemplified, as we saw, in the life of Christ himself, especially in his friendship with Peter, James and John and with Mary, Martha and Lazarus at Bethany.

We see it, too, in the lives of the apostles, especially Paul, who seems never to travel alone, but to be accompanied by one or other of the many friends mentioned in his epistles: Barnabas, John Mark, Silas, Luke, Timothy,

Titus, Epaphroditus. Paul constantly makes clear the debt he owes to these men and to the women who 'contended at my side in the cause of the gospel' (Phil. 4:3). These friendships were not a form of sinful self-indulgence. They were, in the best sense of the word, natural, meeting a need which God has implanted in the very depths of our nature.

Living in community

The same social impulse, reflecting the divine image, is important for understanding our relations with the wider community. God did not intend us to live like hermits on desert islands. Neither would he approve of the current obsession with 'getting away from it all'. Tribes, nations and states are his creation (although we must insist, over against the many forms of nationalism in the world today, that their boundaries are by no means sacrosanct. They were meant to unite people, not to divide them, far less to lead them to commit acts of terrorism against each other). Nor has God anything against cities. Heaven is not described as a nature reserve, far less a wilderness, but as the city of God (Rev. 21:2, 10). Nor have we as Christians any right simply to live among others detached, uninterested, and obsessed only with our own privacy. We are called to bring to bear upon community life all the insights of the gospel, warming that community with the love of Jesus, invigorating it with the power of the Spirit and making it fresh and exciting with the salt of the Christian difference.

A life lived apart from community is a life that violates human nature. We need the nearness, sympathy and counsel of our own kind. Without it, we become neurotic. To refuse it is to show that we are already neurotic.

On the other hand, political and economic conditions can sometimes make true community life impossible and this has an important bearing on the vocation of politicians. Their responsibility, as defined by the New Testament, includes ensuring that men and women can lead honourable and worthwhile lives. Such lives are possible only in a community where, on the one hand, individuality is protected and, on the other, provision is made for as much sharing, participation and interaction as possible. Which means? That those who lead keep those who are led fully informed; that those who have surplus share with those in need; that the population as a whole has a meaningful part in decision-making; and that social mobility is not restricted by artificial barriers of class or rigid immigration laws.

Order and authority

Equality, diversity, community: all of these are reflections of the fact that we bear the image of God. Can we say the same of *order* in human society? For example, does a parent's authority over a child (or a husband's authority over a wife) reflect a similar order in the Trinity, whereby the Father is first, the Son is second and the Spirit is third?

We certainly cannot dismiss the idea out of hand. Jesus himself said, 'The Father is greater than I' (John 14:28), and in the very verse where Paul says, 'the head of every man is Christ, and the head of the woman is man', he also says, 'the head of Christ is God' (1 Cor. 11:3). We must bear in mind, however, that Christ is not *only* divine. He became *man* and took the position of a servant; and some things are true of him as man and as servant which are not true of him as God. As God, he was equal with the Father (Phil. 2:6). As servant, he was subordinate, answerable and dependent. The whole glory of his love is that he was willing to take such a position: to make himself nothing, as Paul puts it (Phil. 2:7).

So far as relations between the persons of the Trinity are concerned, we probably have no right to speak of order or authority. As we saw earlier, the New Testament writers do not regard the order *Father, Son and Holy Spirit* as sacrosanct. As the so-called Athanasian Creed reminds us, 'In this Trinity none is before, or after another: none is greater, or less than another'. Besides, it is a fact that the Bible never appears to ground the order it insists on for human life in relations between the persons of the Trinity.

Our submission to government for example, is based on the fact that government is God's servant (Rom. 13:4). When it comes to the authority of the husband over the wife the Bible mentions several reasons, but none of them has any connection with an order in the depths of the Godhead. Paul and Peter cite, instead, such things as that the man was created first (1 Tim. 2:13), that it was the woman who was deceived (1 Tim. 2:14), that the woman was created for the man, not the man for the woman

(1 Cor. 11:9), and that the woman is the weaker vessel (1 Pet. 3:7). We must not forget, of course, that the husband's authority, whatever its precise extent, always involves corresponding obligations. If he behaves tyrannically and selfishly, he has no right to claim support from the Bible. The very passage (Eph. 5:22-33) which tells the wife to 'obey' also tells the husband to love, nourish and cherish – which surely includes giving the wife scope to express herself and to develop her own talents.

5

Our Life As The Church

More than once the New Testament relates the life of the church very closely to the triune life of God. We see this particularly in John 17:21, where the Lord prays, 'that all of them may be one, Father, just as you are in me and I am in you. May they also be in us so that the world may believe that you have sent me.'

These words remind us how important it was to Christ that his church should be united. They also remind us that what he wanted was not some invisible, inward, spiritual unity, but a oneness the world could *see* and which would convey to it something of the healing and saving power of Christianity. The harmony of mankind had been broken by sin. Everywhere, there were barriers: between Jew and Gentile, between Greek and barbarian, between bond and free. Today things are no better. 'The dividing walls of hostility' (Eph. 2:14) are as high as ever, separating East from West, North from South, rich from poor, black from white, Unionist from Republican. Broken homes, divided communities, gangs and ghettos abound.

The Lord meant his church to be a visible alternative. It was to be a society within which the dividing walls had been broken down and where men and women would not be judged 'according to the flesh' (the colour of their skin, their IQ, the school they went to, the car they owned, their suntans, their weight or where they went on holiday). In the church as the Lord wants it to be, rich and poor, black and white, Asian and Anglo-Saxon sit down together. Its members welcome one another on the basis of spiritual realities, not human characteristics. Here the feeble-minded find acceptance, the easily tempted find strength and the homosexual is helped to put his past behind him.

Imitating God's unity

But what kind of unity is it meant to be? The kind that existed between the Father and the Son: 'that they may be one, just as you are in me and I am in you'. This obviously involves such things as agreement in beliefs and commitment to common objectives. But it also involves much more. We are one because we all have the same relationship with God. All God's children are our brothers and sisters. We don't choose them. God chooses them. Our responsibility is only to love and acknowledge them.

But we must go deeper still. Christians are one in the Father, the Son and the Holy Spirit. We are bound together by the Trinity. In fact, part of the very meaning of being a Christian is that the triune God has taken up residence in each of us. We have the life of God in our souls. Christ lives in us. This is surely something of enormous weight. The triune God does not just *command* us to be 'one', giving his own unity as the model for ours. He actually *makes* us one by dwelling in each of us. How can a Christian hate another human being in whom his very own God and Saviour lives? How can he denigrate him? How can he shoot him?

United in nature

Other things follow. Just as the persons of the Trinity are one in *nature*, so are Christians. They are born again in the image of Christ and share the same primary instincts. They are hungry and thirsty for righteousness (Matt. 5:6). They desire the nourishing milk of God's Word (1 Peter 2:2). They crave the fellowship of God (Ps. 42:1). Their hearts make music to the Lord (Eph. 5:19-20).

United in love

The unity of the church is also one of mutual *love*. We cannot love God, whom we have not seen, without also loving our brother, whom we have (1 John 4:20). Furthermore, God also provides the standard for that love. Before love ever existed in mankind, it existed in God, in the love of the Father for the Son and of both for the Spirit. We are to love our fellow Christians with the same sort of love: 'that the love you have for me may be in them' (John 17:26).

That, surely, is awe-inspiring enough. Do I love other believers the way God the Father loves God the Son? But there is something even more awesome: we are to emulate the depth of love that God the Father showed for *the world* when he gave his only Son for it (John 3:16). Even when our fellow Christians are disappointing, even when they are hurtful, we are to love them in such a way that no sacrifice is too great and no kindness too extravagant. This is not a counsel of perfection or an ideal which is utterly unattainable. It is what Paul had in mind in his great hymn on love in 1 Corinthians 13. No matter how deep our knowledge, how great our gifts, how stupendous our experiences, if we do not show this sort of love our Christianity is mere posturing.

United in ministry

The unity involves, too, mutual *ministry*. One of the most beautiful aspects of the Gospels is the way they reveal the Father and the Spirit ministering to the Son. In fact, this was prophesied in the Old Testament promises of the Messiah. In Isaiah 42:1, for example, God announces: 'Here is my servant, *whom I uphold*, my chosen one in whom I delight; I will put my Spirit on him and he will bring justice to the nations'.

The way this promise was fulfilled was illustrated at Jesus' baptism, when the Spirit visibly descended upon the Lord, and the Father simultaneously encouraged him by acknowledging, 'You are my Son, whom I love; with you I am well pleased' (Mark 1:10-11). After the temptation, God sent angels to attend to him (Mark 1:13). He did the same again during Jesus' agony in Gethsemane (Luke 22:43). Just before the Passion, God strengthened him on the Mount of Transfiguration with another word of reassurance: 'This is my Son, whom I love. Listen to him!' (Mark 9:7). Throughout Jesus' ministry, God was accrediting him by means of miracles, wonders and signs (Acts 2:22). The writer to the Hebrews tells us that it was through the eternal Spirit that Jesus offered himself to God (Heb. 9:14); and Jesus makes plain his own appreciation of the help he was receiving when he says in John 8:16: 'I am not alone. I stand with the Father, who sent me'.

This concern for the Son on the part of the Father and the Spirit is a model for the way believers should serve one another. It is a ministry of consolation and encouragement. How important, for example, it can sometimes be just to recognise one another: to say, 'My brother!' or 'My sister!' as the Father said, 'My Son!'; to say, at least occasionally, 'I am well pleased!' We should say it as individuals, to one another; and we should say it as denominations, one branch of Christ's church recognising and encouraging another. Too often we speak to one another only when the occasion calls for rebuke and criticism. The account we have of relations between the Son and the other persons of the Godhead during his earthly ministry indicates that they were totally involved in his ministry and fully committed to him. That is how it should be between the various members of the church.

United in fellowship

It is clear, too, that the unity between the Father, the Son and the Spirit involves the fullest possible *fellowship*. The New Testament word for this is *koinonia* which means *sharing* or *having in common*. At the deepest level this fellowship between the persons of the Trinity means that they share the same nature. They have the one divine *being* in common (this, as we saw, is what the church fathers expressed in the word *homoousios*). The Father, the Son and the Holy Spirit also share equally in the divine *sovereignty*. This is expressed symbolically in Revelation 5:6 where the Son sits with the Father in the centre of the throne. They share, too, the same *glory*. The Son's glory is a glory *with* the Father (John 17:5). The same is true of the divine *knowledge*. Whatever the Father knows, the Spirit and the Son also know. We see this in, for example, Matthew 11:27. There are things which have been hidden from the wise and prudent but have been revealed to Christ: 'All things have been committed to me by my Father'. The Father, the Son and the Spirit keep nothing hidden from one another. In fact, the Lord can even say: 'All I have is yours, and all you have is mine' (John 17:10).

This sharing is to be reflected in relations between Christians. In his first letter, John tells us that 'we have fellowship with one another' (1 John 1:7). We share everything. We share the work of evangelism (Phil 1:5).

We share in giving and receiving (Phil 4:15-16). We share gifts, all of which belong to the whole body (1 Cor. 12:7). We bear one another's burdens (Gal. 6:2). We share in such a way as to ensure that no fellow Christian is in need (Acts 4:34-35).

All this is brought out in the Lord's Supper, which is why it is often called 'Communion'. Paul calls it a participation in the body of Christ and in the blood of Christ (1 Cor. 10:16). This does not mean that such a participation occurs *only* in the sacrament. The Lord's Supper, at least at this point, is highlighting something which is true of our entire Christian lives. We are bound together by the fact that, *wherever* we are, we are sharing in the body and blood of Christ: that is, we are experiencing together the blessings of the new covenant (blessings which have been secured by the breaking of the Lord's body and the shedding of his blood).

As far as possible this fact should be expressed in the way we administer the sacrament. If we receive the bread from an ordinary fellow believer, and pass it on to the next, this expresses the truth that the church is a fellowship of giving and receiving, in which God's gifts are in constant circulation and in which everyone has something to give as well as something to receive. If anything clutters up this circulation, the whole church suffers.

'One flesh'

But there is something beyond fellowship and deeper even than fellowship. The great theologians of the early church had a special word for it, *perichoresis,* but unfortunately it is very difficult to translate into English. What they were trying to say was this. The persons of the Trinity are not only *beside, with* and *towards* one another: they dwell *in* each other. We see this in John 14:11, 'I am *in* the Father and the Father is *in* me'. It also occurs in John 17:21, 'that all of them may be one, Father, just as you are *in* me and I am *in* you'; and again in John 17:23, 'I *in* them and you *in* me'. Words such as these suggest a kind of union and interpenetration which is incredibly close and intimate, far beyond anything we can experience as human beings. This is why in John 14:9, Jesus can say to Philip, 'Anyone who has seen me has seen the Father'.

It is obviously impossible for us to have such a close relationship with any other human being. Yet in the Christian church, conceived of as the body of Christ, there is something more than mere sharing. There is such an involvement with one another and such a depth of affection and sympathy, that 'if one part suffers, every part suffers with it' (1 Cor. 12:26). Similarly, if one Christian is not performing his proper function, all are affected, because the church is a body, joined and held together by every supporting ligament, and it can grow only when each part does its work (Eph. 4:16).

We have no right to be in each other's way and even less to be in each other's hair. Yet the passages we have just quoted from the New Testament reflect a degree of commitment, concern, involvement and intimacy far beyond what we usually find in churches today. The fact that Christ and the church are 'one flesh' (Eph. 5:29-32) indicates not simply a close bond between him and each of the other members of the body, but also a very close bond between the various members themselves. They, too, are one flesh, deeply involved in each other, and they must express this in their collective lifestyle.

Imitating God's diversity

Enough has been said, one hopes, to establish the importance of the doctrine of the Trinity for the unity of the church. But it is no less important for the church's diversity. We have seen that the Father, the Son and the Spirit are clearly distinct. Each is different. Each has his own unique quality which gives him his personal identity. If the church is to reflect the life of the Trinity it must do justice to this diversity. We are not only to concede that Christians are all different. We are to insist on it and even to revel and take pride in it. The worldwide church reflects an astonishing variety of nationalities, cultures, intelligence, insights, temperaments, aptitudes and experience. The church of one age differs from that of another. Each has its own character, reflecting the circumstances in which it came into being, its history, its environment and its leadership.

One implication of this is that what God wants of each of us is *our* service. We see this in the way the apostles identified themselves when they wrote to the early churches. They did not say, 'This is an apostle speaking'. They said, 'This is Peter speaking' or, 'This is John speaking'. We are ourselves, and our service must reflect what we are and what we are capable of. For some of us, to equal others would be impossible. For others, it would not be enough. From each of us, God wants our whole life: a sacrifice which expresses what we are by heredity, by environment, by the experience of grace and by the gifts of the Spirit.

In the same way, the various regional churches and the various Christian denominations have different contributions to make to the work of God's kingdom. Some are strong theologically, others are strong in missionary gifts, and yet others strong in the patient endurance of suffering. It is for God himself to weave these various threads into a common tapestry. But no tapestry can come out of bland uniformity. Our national and cultural distinctions give colour to our Christian service.

We must be careful not to set this unity and this diversity over against each other. The church is not one *despite* its diversity but *because* of its diversity. Think again of the body. Each of us has one body, but it is made up of many different parts. It functions as a unit only if it has the necessary bits and pieces and only if each does its proper job. The same is true of a car. It would not be much use if it were all clutch or if the gear-box tried to be a carburettor. Of course we cannot press such illustrations too far. Tonsils and oesophaguses, clutches and carburettors, do not have the perverseness and stubbornness of many church members!

It remains true, however, that the unity of the Godhead results from the Father being the Father, the Son being the Son and the Spirit being the Spirit. In the same way, the unity of the church results from each one of us being himself or herself and doing what God has designed us for. What destroys Christian unity is not lack of uniformity but the absence of what we may call 'unifying power': love for God, love for each other and shared concern for the world. If we lack these, we turn in upon ourselves destructively. If we have them, we forget personal needs and interests and get on with expressing in our own distinctive way our obedience to Christ.

6

The Trinity and
The Christian Life

God in us

When we come to reflect on the bearing of the doctrine of the Trinity on our personal Christian lives one fact stands out above all others: the three persons of the eternal Trinity live in every Christian. They have taken up residence in his or her being. Our bodies are temples of God (1 Cor 6:19). The Lord refers to this in John 14:23, reminding us that not only himself but also God the Father lives in us: 'If anyone loves me, he will obey my teaching. My Father will love him, and we will come to him and make our home with him'. John's first letter also teaches that God the Father lives within us. In 1 John 4:12, 16, for example, we read: 'If we love one another, God lives in us and his love is made complete in us... Whoever lives in love lives in God, and God in him'.

The New Testament often emphasises that Christ lives in us. We read in John 14:18, for example, 'I will not leave you as orphans; I will come to you'. There is similar teaching in John 15:4-5: 'Remain in me, and I will remain in you .... If a man remains in me and I in him, he will bear much fruit'. Paul stresses the same thing, telling the Galatians, 'I have been crucified with Christ and I no longer live, but Christ lives in me' (Gal. 2:20). One of his prayers for the Ephesians was 'that Christ may dwell in your hearts through faith' (Eph. 3:17).

The fact that the Holy Spirit lives in us is brought out even more often. According to Romans 8:11, the Spirit of him who raised Jesus from the dead is living in us; according to John 14:17 he lives with us and will be in us; and according to Acts 2:4, he fills us. Various other passages speak of our being baptised in the Spirit (Acts 1:5), led by the Spirit (Rom. 8:14) and helped by the Spirit (Rom. 8:26).

The obvious conclusion from all this is that the Christian is a quite extraordinary person. If we were to say that he is someone walking about with God inside him we would not be all that far wrong. Henry Scougal was certainly right to speak of 'the life of God in the soul of man'.

But what does this imply?

Implications

First, *security*. We are guarded by the power of God (1 Pet. 1:5). Many things seek to corrupt and destroy us, but inside us there is this invincible garrison, the triune God. God is a shield (Ps. 84:11), a mighty fortress (Ps. 18:2) and a hiding place (Ps. 32:7). We are safe because the real springs of our lives are hidden in God (Col. 3:3) beyond the reach of any enemy.

Secondly, the indwelling of the triune God means *power*. The Bible makes some astonishing statements in this connection. Take, for example, the words of Isaiah 40:29-31. In situations where fit and strong, battle-hardened warriors are defeated and give up, poor and inadequate people who wait on God experience renewal of strength: 'They will soar on wings like eagles; they will run and not grow weary, they will walk and not be faint.'

There is similar teaching in Romans 8:37. Among all the distractions of famine and persecution, hardship and danger, we not only conquer, we *more* than conquer. We are hyper-conquerors, super-conquerors. It is not a matter of bare survival. It is a matter of triumphant victory.

In Philippians 4:13, Paul seems to carry this even further: 'I can do everything through him who gives me strength.'

He does not say who exactly gives him strength. He leaves it open: 'the strengthening one'. But in the light of what we have already seen there is no need to decide whether he is referring to the Father, to the Son or to the

Holy Spirit. The triune God strengthens us. What really matters is the result: 'I can do everything'. What is on Paul's mind at the precise moment of writing is contentment. Even in a Roman prison, he can be content (Phil. 4:12). In fact, he can be content 'in any and every situation'. How? In the strengthening one! In him, Paul can do everything. Christians can do anything God wants them to do. They can carry any burden, overcome any temptation, endure any pain. God meets all their needs.

This must be the stuff of our dreams. There is nothing the church and the Christian cannot do, if we prayerfully set our minds to it. Our own inherent gifts and strength are not at all the measure of our potential. God, dwelling in us by his Spirit, is the measure.

In her famous interview with Michael Parkinson, Commissioner Catherine Bramwell-Booth recounted how, as a young girl, she returned one day to her local Salvation Army Headquarters after sharing in a service. There, before her, was her grandfather, the formidable General Booth. 'How did you get on, Catherine?' he asked, intimidatingly. 'I did my best, gran'pa,' she replied meekly. The General's response was devastating: 'Catherine, your best is not good enough!' But he added: 'In Christ, we can do better than our best'. That is what it means to be indwelt by the triune God.

There is, however, a more sombre side to this great truth that God lives in us: *we can never escape from his presence.* We can never shake him off. In part, this means that we cannot ask God to turn his back while we sin.

Since our bodies are themselves his temple, the only place where we can sin is in his temple, under his very nose. There is something claustrophobic about this, which is why in Psalm 139 we have the extraordinary spectacle of a believer wanting to get away from God:

> *'You hem me in, behind and before;*
> *you have laid your hand upon me.*
> *Where can I go from your Spirit?*
> *Where can I flee from your presence?'*

Psalm 139:5, 7

To make matters worse, this God who is present is in the highest degree formidable: 'Our God is a consuming fire' (Heb. 12:29). This point is made very forcibly in the story of Pentecost, when God came to dwell in a special way with his people. He comes as a violent wind and in tongues of fire (Acts 2:2, 3) – not at all cosy and easy to live with. The God who came upon the apostolic church came as a powerful (and sometimes as a violent) force, rushing through the world conquering and transforming.

But, equally, he came as fire: and whatever else fire is, it is dangerous. Even the slightest acquaintance with the Old Testament makes plain how difficult it was to be an Israelite. God lived with them and that brought many blessings. But it brought much else besides. It was like having the Admiral aboard ship all the time. Other nations could get away with things. But not Israel. It seemed to have far more 'rules' than the other nations.

Besides, God was constantly 'visiting': and by no means always to bless them.

The same was true in the New Testament: something that Ananias and Sapphira forgot (Acts 5:1-11). They pretended they had given more to the Lord's work than they actually had. They lied to God and the consequences were dire. No wonder that 'great fear seized the whole church and all who heard about these events' (Acts 5:11).

The presence of God in and with his people is indeed a great comfort and encouragement. But it also applies real pressure. The very fact that he lives among us gives particular force to the commandment, 'Be holy, because I am holy' (1 Peter 1:16; Lev. 11:44-45). We cannot deceive God. We cannot trifle with him. And we cannot sin, undetected.

Adoption

One special blessing of the Christian life is *adoption*, and we can certainly understand this properly only in the light of the Trinity. In adoption, believers become sons and daughters of God, which means that they come to share in the very relationship with God enjoyed by Jesus. There are, of course, some differences, as the Lord's own language sometimes indicates. In John 20:17, for example, he avoids saying '*our* Father' and says instead: 'I am returning to my Father and your Father, to my God and your God'.

But the difference is a matter of *the way* we become his children, rather than of what the relationship itself means.

Christ is God's Son eternally: we become God's sons and daughters only when we receive Jesus (John 1:12). He is God's Son by nature: we become God's children by grace (1 John 3:1). But the relationship itself is essentially the same. We are heirs of God and *co-heirs* with Christ (Rom. 8:17). We have exactly the same inheritance. According to John 17:26, we are also loved with the same love: 'that the love you have for me may be in them and that I myself may be in them'. Like Jesus, too, we have the right to call God, 'Abba!' (Father), something the Jews before Christ never did. We have a right to go to the very throne of God, approach the King in person frankly and confidently, and discuss with him everything that intrigues or troubles us (Heb. 4:16).

Most remarkably of all, Jesus' destiny and ours are to be the same. At one point he says, 'Father, I want those you have given me to be with me where I am, and to see my glory, the glory you have given me' (John 17:24). At another point what he says is this: 'I have given them the glory that you gave me' (John 17:22). And in John 14:3 he assures the disciples: 'And if I go and prepare a place for you, I will come back and take you to be with me that you also may be where I am'.

Have we any idea what this means in detail? For one thing, we are to have *bodies* identical to the resurrection body of Christ. Paul assures us of this in Philippians 3:21: The Lord 'will transform our lowly bodies so that they will be like his glorious body'. In the same way, God will transform our *characters and personalities*. In fact, this is why he chose and called us, 'to be conformed to the likeness of his Son' (Romans 8:29). In this respect, divine adoption differs radically from human. Human adoptive parents can lavish all kinds of love and generosity on their children. But they cannot change them internally because many characteristics are inherited. An adopted child is not going to have his adoptive father's blue eyes or his adoptive mother's intelligence. But when God adopts he also *transforms* so that at last we are totally Christ-like.

In the same way, we share the eternal Son's position and eminence. God intended us to 'rule over the fish of the sea and the birds of the air, over the livestock, over all the earth, and over all the creatures that move along the ground' (Gen. 1:26). Only in Christ do we fulfil that destiny (Heb. 2:6-9). We reign *with him* (2 Tim. 2:11-12). He even shares his environment with us, taking us to the very place he has gone to himself (John 14:3) and letting us come so close that we can see him face to face (1 Cor. 13:12).

All this means is that in redemption the idea of fellowship with Christ is carried to the most extravagant lengths. The result (and intention) of the love shown by the Father in giving his Son is that we enjoy 'eternal life': that is, we share in the life of God himself. Every blessing Christ enjoys as Son is ours. It is as if in the church everyone had rights of *primogeniture* (this is probably why, in Heb. 12:23, the church is called 'the church of the firstborn').

We must not forget, however, that there is a darker side to this, too: what Paul calls 'sharing in his sufferings'

(Phil 3:10). Christ, God's firstborn and our elder brother, was made perfect through suffering (Heb. 2:10). He was hated by the world, forsaken by his friends and attacked by the devil. He knew the extremes of both physical and emotional pain. Christians will inevitably share in this; and even if we in the Western world have for the moment a comparatively easy existence, we must not forget the millions of our fellow believers, particularly in Marxist and Muslim countries, for whom discipleship is still costly. They know what the New Testament church meant when it said, 'If we endure, we will also reign with him' (2 Tim. 2:12).

Evangelism

At first sight there is little connection between the doctrine of the Trinity and evangelism. If we look a little more closely, however, we may find that things are not quite as they appear.

For example, in the great commission, Jesus told his disciples to 'make disciples of all nations, baptising them in the name of the Father and of the Son and of the Holy Spirit' (Matt. 28:19). It is hardly likely that they were baptised into a name of which they were completely ignorant; implicit in the commission was the command to *teach* all nations about the Father, Son and Holy Spirit.

According to Acts 8:37, the Ethiopian eunuch was baptised as one who believed that Jesus is the Son of God (this verse is found only in late manuscripts, but the tradition of the Ethiopian's confession of faith in Christ was current as early as the second century).

In Acts 2:38, after explaining that God the Father raised Jesus from the dead and gave him the Holy Spirit, Peter appeals to the crowd to be baptised in the name of Jesus Christ.

Again, when the jailer in Acts 16:30 asks what he must do to be saved, Paul's reply is, 'Believe in the Lord Jesus'. Before he and his household are baptised, Paul teaches them this about the Lord. In the New Testament, becoming a Christian meant coming to believe in the lordship of Jesus, the love of the Father and the baptism of the Spirit. In such a situation, there could be no such thing as un-theological evangelism. There could be no faith without hearing. But by the same token, faith could not be kept to oneself. The truth that Jesus was Lord, that God was his Father and that the Spirit was his delegate was not meant only for the closet or the classroom. It was truth for personal witness, open-air preaching, tract distribution and evangelistic rallies.

In fact, without this doctrine, we cannot even begin to understand the promises Jesus makes in the Gospels. Take just one of these, Matthew 11:28, where the Lord says, 'Come to me, all you who are weary and burdened, and I will give you rest'. These are familiar words. But their familiarity should not blind us to their extraordinary nature. He invites the whole world (no less!) to come to him and he promises, 'Suppose they *all* come, I can give them all rest. I can teach them all. I can carry the burdens of them all. I can meet their deepest needs. I can deliver them from every neurosis and every anxiety and make them whole and free'. Without the doctrine of the Trinity, and its recognition of Jesus as divine, these are the words of a raving megalomaniac. Only because his resources of love and wisdom and power are infinite can the Saviour deliver on a promise so vast and full.

It also follows that it is what Jesus is, as set forth in the doctrine of the Trinity, that gives us the real reason for coming to him in faith. Why should we become Christians? Too often people give the impression that they turned to Christ because they had come to some crisis or they were up against a wall or they were in the midst of some great loss and their lives were empty: and so they surrendered to Jesus. Apart from everything else this suggests that if you aren't in a jam, and you're coping OK with life, there's no reason whatever for becoming a Christian.

In fact, the real reason for becoming a Christian is surely Jesus himself. Whatever we feel or don't feel, need or don't need, he is Lord, and that's why we bow the knee. Suppose we *are* managing just fine, leading ordinary, decent lives, holding down good jobs, going with a steady boyfriend and guilty of no particular evil habits, we should still be Christians. Why? Because he's there! Because he's God! Because it's true! We worship – we fall at his feet – not because of what we feel but quite simply because of who and what he is.

Worship

Which brings us back to the most important of all the practical implications of the doctrine of the Trinity: we must worship God *as triune.*

Probably the mental image most Christians have of the Trinity is of a large throne surrounded by two little ones: the Father in the centre and the Son and the Spirit sitting like little princes, one on the right hand and one on the left. This image is certainly reflected in much Christian worship, which tends to be directed exclusively to God the Father. If, however, the Son and Spirit are one with the Father and in the fullest sense divine, they must have an equal place in our adoration. In the New Testament, actual references to worshipping the Spirit are rare, although we are warned not to *grieve* him (Eph. 4:30) and the consequences of offending him are made clear in the story of Ananias and Sapphira (Acts 5:1-11). On the other hand, whatever reasons we have for believing that the Spirit is God are also reasons for worshipping him. As the Creed reminds us, if he is the same in nature with the Father and the Son, then, with them, he must be worshipped and glorified:

> *Dwell, therefore, in our hearts,*
> *Our minds from bondage free:*
> *Then shall we know and praise and love*
> *The Father, Son and Thee.*

Joseph Hart

With regard to the Son, by contrast, there is much direct evidence that the early church worshipped him. This is true even of the period before his cross and resurrection. In Matthew 2:2, for example, the Magi announce that they have come to worship him, and in Luke 5:8 we see Peter falling on his knees before Jesus and saying, 'Go away from me, Lord; I am a sinful man!' Immediately after the resurrection, Matthew reports, the disciples 'clasped his feet and worshipped him' (Matt. 28:9). In 1 Corinthians 1:2, Christians are defined precisely as worshippers of Jesus: 'those everywhere who call on the name of our Lord Jesus Christ'. In 2 Corinthians 12:8, Paul recounts that when he was tormented by 'the thorn in his flesh' it was with *the Lord* (Jesus) that he pleaded three times to take it away. In Ephesians 5:19, he describes Christian worshippers not only as those who give thanks to God the Father but also as those who 'sing and make music in [their] heart to the Lord'. In Philippians 2:10 we are told that at last every knee will bow at the name of Jesus and every tongue will confess that he is Lord. According to Hebrews 1:6, all God's angels are to worship him, and according to Revelation 1:17, our instinctive response if we could see him would be to fall at his feet as though dead.

In fact, this worshipping of Jesus seems to have been the most obvious thing about early Christians so far as the pagans were concerned. One of the earliest references to Christians in secular sources is in a letter (written about 112 A.D.) from the Roman bureaucrat, Pliny, to the Emperor Trajan. Pliny describes the Christians accustomed to meet on an appointed day at daybreak 'to sing a hymn to Christ, as to a god'.

For us today, this remains the most important thing: we worship God the Son equally with God the Father. He evokes the same love, awakens the same sense of the holy and inspires the same trust and confidence. To him, no less than the Father, we direct our prayers. To him we sing our hymns and doxologies. It is his Word we hear in preaching and his name we bless in the Eucharist. To him we offer instant, unconditional obedience. For him, we lose our lives: 'Anyone who loves his father or mother more than me is not worthy of me; anyone who loves his son or daughter more than me is not worthy of me; and anyone who does not take his cross and follow me is not worthy of me. Whoever finds his life will lose it, and whoever loses his life for my sake will find it' (Matt. 10:37-39).

Praise and honour to the Father,
Praise and honour to the Son,
Praise and honour to the Spirit,
Ever three and ever one;
One in power and one in glory
While eternal ages run.

J. M Neale, altered by Jubilate Hymns

PART 3

Under Attack

7

Judaism and Islam

Not surprisingly, the doctrine of the Trinity has been rejected and ridiculed not only by out-and-out pagans but by many deeply religious people and even by some who claim to be Christians. We will look first at the two theistic religions which share with Christianity a belief in one God.

Judaism

To Jews, the whole idea of a triune God is utterly abhorrent. In the early Christian centuries they could speak of Jesus only with contempt, dismissing him as a sorcerer and imposter. Recently they have spoken more respectfully, recognising at least the worth of his moral teaching. But Judaism still rejects what to Christians are the most important claims of Jesus: that he was Messiah and that he was the Son of God. In fact no one could believe either of these doctrines and still expect to be accepted as a Jew, no matter how loyal he was to other traditions of his race. As one famous Jew, Martin Buber, put it: 'Whoever regards Jesus as a historical personality, be he ever so high, may belong to us, but he who acknowledges Jesus to be the Messiah already come, cannot belong to us'.

What lies behind this Jewish rejection of Jesus as God?

Messiahship

Take the messiahship first. As Jews see it, there are at least four good reasons for refusing Jesus' claim.

The death he died

First, the death he suffered. Not only did he die, he died ignominiously: in the eyes of the Romans, as a convicted terrorist; in the eyes of the Jews, as a blasphemer. Even worse, he was executed in a manner which the Jews had always regarded as cursed: 'anyone who is hung on a tree is under God's curse' (Deut. 21:23). And as if all this were not bad enough, he himself confessed with his dying breath that he was abandoned by God: 'My God, my God, why have you forsaken me?' (Mark 15:34).

But if this argument is really as strong as Jews contend, their rejection of Jesus should be outright and total. In this respect the early Jewish attitude was more consistent than today's. There can be no half-measures with someone cursed by God. It is certainly quite improper for worshippers of that God to extol the victim's virtues. He should be left 'outside the camp' where all accursed things belong. The fact that having pronounced Christ cursed they then go on to make concessions, even praising his virtues and commending him as a fine example, shows that they don't accept the cross as the final word.

It is curious, too, if the cross is so decisive against Jesus, that the early Christians put it in the very forefront of their message. We find this already in one of the earliest books of the New Testament, Paul's letter to the Galatians: 'May I never boast except in the cross of our Lord Jesus Christ' (Gal. 6:14). But the trend did not begin with Paul. According to Acts 2:23 Peter did the same thing on the day of Pentecost: 'This man was handed over to you by God's set purpose and foreknowledge; and you, with the help of wicked men, put him to death by nailing him to the cross.' In fact, according to the Gospels this emphasis on the cross goes right back to Jesus himself. Matthew, Mark and Luke all report him as teaching that the very reason he came into the world was 'to give his life as a ransom for many' (Mark 10:45).

In effect, the early Christians (and Christians ever since) were boasting about what, according to Jews, they ought to have been ashamed of. Why was this? For one thing, they could point to what they thought were clear indications in the Old Testament that the Messiah was to be not only a glorious but also a humiliated figure. For example, when Christ exclaimed that he was forsaken by God he was only quoting words used by David, Israel's great king, in Psalm 22:1. Was this a sign that David was rejected by God? And if the coming Messiah was to be another David, only greater, why should such typical experiences of his predecessor be forbidden to him?

Then there was 'the Suffering Servant' spoken of so often by the prophet Isaiah. According to Jews, of course, the Servant was the nation Israel (an interpretation also accepted by many modern Christian scholars). But the objections to this are formidable. It is very difficult to fit it into what Isaiah actually says. In the prophecy, the Jews are those to whom he preached his message: and who refused to hear it. Far from being the Servant, they rejected God's word about the Servant (Isa. 53:1).

Again, do the Jews really accept that *they* are without beauty or majesty or attractiveness (Isa. 53:2)? Is it true historically that the Jews suffered uncomplainingly (Isa. 53:7)? Can they claim to be sinless, like the Servant (Isa. 53:9)? Above all, can they claim that their suffering has been in the place of others; that it has atoned for the sins of others; or that it has brought peace and healing to others? All these things are said of the sufferings of the Servant (Isa 53:4-6).

By contrast, when we take Isaiah's words as referring to Jesus, we find a remarkable correspondence between what the prophet foretold and what Christ actually suffered. He was despised and rejected. He was judged to be totally irrelevant and unattractive. He was a man of sorrows. He was judged to be cursed by God himself. He was pierced, bruised and beaten: meek and silent before his tormentors.

The Christian interpretation fits the actual word of the prophet. Whatever the Jews came to expect, the Messiah foretold by the prophets was not to be simply imperious, honoured and glorious. He was to be a humble servant who would experience rejection and suffering. The Jews had a long tradition of turning upon those God sent to lead and teach them. They had done it to Moses, to David and to virtually all the great prophets. The Messiah was to be no exception. He would be the capping stone rejected by the builders (Ps. 118:22; 1 Peter 2:7).

The apostles, however, saw that these sufferings were actually the fulfilment of what was predicted of the Messiah. What's more, they, and all Christians since, saw the sufferings of Christ as an essential part of God's plan of salvation. Jesus' sacrifice was the atonement provided by God for man's sin. So far as Christ himself was concerned, this was the real reason for his coming into the world. He came to give his life as a ransom for many (Mark 10:45). This is certainly how the New Testament portrays his death: not as an accident or a tragedy or a martyrdom, but as a sacrifice, agreed between the Father and the Son, which made up for man's disobedience against God. Seen from this point of view the cross, far from being meaningless, was the supreme expression of God's love for the world (John 3:16).

Unfortunately, modern Jews will have none of it. They claim, for example, that the story of Abraham and Isaac (Gen. 22:1-19) shows that God forbids human sacrifice. But surely it proves the very opposite? God would not have commanded the patriarch to do something intrinsically wrong. In fact, when John the Baptist called out, 'Look, the Lamb of God!' (John 1:36) he was probably alluding to Abraham's very words in Genesis 22:8, 'God himself will provide the lamb for the burnt offering.'

The whole idea of a sacrifice for sin is abhorrent to Jews. As far as they are concerned, there is no such thing as original sin; and for actual sins, repentance is an adequate atonement. As one leading Jewish teacher puts it: 'If by straying from the right path man lapses into sin, regret and penitence will repair the ravages of his transgression and will restore the harmony between him and his Creator' (Isidore Epstein, *Judaism*, Penguin, 1979, p. 142).

This, however, reveals a modern Judaism that is completely different from the Judaism of the Old Testament. The exodus itself, the birth of the nation, depended on the sacrifice of the Passover; and the life of the nation depended on the unending ritual of daily, weekly, monthly and annual sacrifices. Every year, there had to be a Day of Atonement. The Suffering Servant himself, whoever he was, was to be a sacrifice: the Lord makes his life a guilt offering (Isa. 53:10). A religion which has no priesthood, offers no sacrifices and lacks any sense of sin, surely has little connection with the religion of the patriarchs, prophets and psalmists.

Conversely, as the writer to the Hebrews points out, it is very difficult to see how these ancient sacrifices ('the blood of goats and bulls and the ashes of a heifer sprinkled on those who are ceremonially unclean', Heb. 9:13) could be any more than symbols and shadows. And so far as their fulfilment is concerned, one can hardly imagine anything more glorious than the Christian doctrine of the atonement, according to which God himself takes our place as man and not only offers, but becomes the sacrifice. True or false, nothing greater (and therefore nothing more Godlike) can be conceived. In this light, the death on Calvary, far from being the disgrace of the Messiah, is his crowning glory.

But the most important thing still remains to be said. God did not allow the cross to be the last word. He raised Christ from the dead. Not that this was the only attestation of Jesus as Messiah. Throughout his life, as Peter reminded his audience at Pentecost (Acts 2:22), God had been accrediting Jesus by a long series of 'miracles, wonders and signs'. And when John the Baptist sent men to ask if Jesus was indeed the Messiah, it was to these 'signs' that Jesus pointed: 'Go back and report to John what you hear and see: The blind receive sight, the lame walk, those who have leprosy are cured, the deaf hear, the dead are raised, and the good news is preached to the poor' (Matt. 11:4ff.).

The resurrection was the supreme attestation of Jesus' messiahship. The cross looked like the end for Jesus. It seemed to express not only the hatred and rejection of men, but also repudiation by God himself. It destroyed the faith of even the disciples. But the resurrection reversed all that. It declared that the grave could not hold him. It vindicated his claims. It proclaimed God's approval. It restored the disciples to a living hope (1 Peter 1:3).

The only way round these conclusions is to deny the resurrection itself: to deny that he was seen by Mary Magdalene, by Peter, by the Eleven and on one occasion by no fewer than 500 disciples (1 Cor. 15:6); to deny Paul's experience on the Damascus Road (Acts 9:4) and the experience of the entire church at Pentecost (Acts 2:33). If Christ has risen, he is the Messiah. If Christ has risen, he is all that Christians claim for him.

The world's Messiah

Secondly, Jews do not regard Jesus as the Messiah, because he rejected the unique position of Israel and claimed to be the Messiah not only of Jews but of the world. He announced that other men were to be admitted to the Kingdom on exactly the same terms as 'the chosen people'. This was something which gave offence from the very beginning of his ministry. When he preached his first sermon in the synagogue of his home town, Nazareth, everybody thought well of him until he went on to speak of God's concern for the wider world, as expressed in Elijah's ministry to the widow of Zarephath and Elisha's to Naaman the Syrian: 'All the people in the synagogue were furious when they heard this. They got up and drove him out of the town' (Luke 4:28-29).

In taking such an attitude, however, Jews, then and now, are again profoundly unfaithful to their own biblical tradition. The very reason for God's calling Abraham was to bring blessing to all nations on earth (Gen. 22:18); and the prophet Joel had foretold that in the new age God would pour his Spirit on all people (Joel 2:28). In proclaiming good news for Gentiles Jesus was doing no more than the Old Testament had promised. Indeed, he was only calling Israel back to its true calling as the channel of blessing to the whole world.

On the other hand, it is not entirely true that Jesus denied the unique position of Israel. Many Christians believe that Israel is still special to God: the Jews are loved on account of the patriarchs (Rom. 11:28). One day God will bring them to see that Jesus is their Messiah, and that event will be of immense benefit both to the church and to the whole world. It will, in short, be nothing less than 'life from the dead' (Rom. 11:15).

No political restoration

Thirdly, Jews reject Jesus because he promised no political restoration. They see the Messiah as the human, mortal offspring of David, called to restore the Davidic throne and rehabilitate Israel politically. This is the precondition of any moral and spiritual influence Israel might have; and in any case the Messianic predictions of the prophets refer exclusively to an *earthly* future.

There is no doubt that this is how the Jews of Jesus' own day saw things too. This is probably why he never referred to himself as the Messiah. The term was too misleading. Even his own disciples cherished the hope of earthly glory. They pressed him to tell them when he would restore the Jewish kingdom (Acts 1:7) and dreamed of occupying positions of splendour and pre-eminence when the glory came (Mark 10:37). Jesus put down all such notions, not only in the matter-of-fact statement, 'My kingdom is not of this world!' but in much more revolutionary disclaimers. He had not come to be served, but to serve (Mark 10:45). In his kingdom, the blessings were spiritual and the King washed his subjects' feet (John 13:5).

Was Jesus' denial of this a betrayal of the original Jewish vision as reflected in the Old Testament? Surely not. The key promise made to Israel was a spiritual one: 'I will be your God' (Gen. 17:7). If the promise was political and economic it was never fulfilled, at least so far as Abraham was concerned. He didn't own even a plot of ground to bury Sarah in. The picture for most of the Old Testament was the same. There were occasional moments of prosperity and national prestige. But for the most part, the life of Israel was one of struggle, poverty, hardship, exile and oppression. This was *particularly* true of the faithful remnant. They were the true heirs of the promise. But they were poor and afflicted. It was the ungodly who were wealthy and powerful.

When the prophets spoke of the future they certainly did not confine themselves to making political promises. The Servant (whether nation or Messiah) would bring peace, righteousness, and healing. He would redeem from iniquity and intercede for transgressors (Isa. 53:5, 11, 12). Amos rebuked his contemporaries for looking forward to the Day of the Lord (the Age of the Messiah) as a time simply of joy and eminence for the Jews. It would, he said, bring darkness, not light. And for Joel, as we have seen, the important thing about the last days was not the establishment of a new Jewish empire but the pouring of the Spirit on all people.

Seen this way, Jesus was not unfaithful to the hope of Israel. It is a matter of opinion which, the Jewish or the Christian, is the more glorious vision. But there is surely much to be said for the idea that he who brings spiritual light, peace and power to men brings more than he who meets the craving for loaves and fishes, or the aspirations of national pride.

On the other hand, the contrast must not be drawn too sharply. During his days on earth Jesus healed bodies as well as cured souls; and according to the Christian hope he provides for physical resurrection as well as for spiritual renewal. The promise that the seed of Abraham will inherit the earth still stands, even though Christian faith extends it to include the meek ones who follow Jesus the Messiah. In Christ, the last Adam, the sons of men will subdue and colonise the earth.

Disrespectful to tradition

Fourthly, Jews argue that Jesus cannot be the Messiah because he was disrespectful towards traditional interpretations of the law. It is compliance with these traditions that gives a Jew his identity, and to annul them is to destroy Judaism as a life force.

It is worth noting, however, that Jesus is not accused of disrespect for the law (Torah) as such. For the Old Testament itself he had the highest regard. He declared that he had not come to destroy the law and the prophets but to fulfil them (Matt. 5:17). He appealed to them constantly when challenged as to his conduct or his teaching. The trouble, as Jesus saw it, was not that the Jews took the law too seriously, but that they did not take it seriously enough. They were nullifying the Word of God by their traditions (Mark 7:13). Christ wanted not something less, but something infinitely more. The Christian's righteousness must *surpass* that of the Pharisees (Matt. 5:20). In fact, the traditions were often only ways round the law. They told you when it was *not* necessary to love; when you *could dissolve* a marriage; and when you could *break* the Sabbath. As far as Jesus was concerned, the command to love *always* applied and every jot and tittle of the law had categorical authority.

The Son of God?

Jews also reject the idea that Jesus is in some unique and special sense the Son of God and therefore divine. They back this rejection, too, with specific arguments.

A late addition

First, they argue that the original Christians did not regard Jesus as divine. They differed from Jews only in accepting him as Messiah (a purely human figure). Only later (through the influence of Paul) did Christians begin to think of him as a divine person. It was this which made the breach with Judaism inevitable.

One obvious difficulty with this is that the breach with Judaism came long before the apostle Paul. It came in the lifetime of Christ himself. He lived in open conflict with the Pharisees, pronounced on them his famous woes (Matt. 23:13-39), and was crucified at their instigation. Furthermore, all the accounts we have of the crucifixion clearly indicate that it took place because the Jews regarded Jesus' claim as blasphemous. We see this clearly in, for example, Mark 14:61ff. At his trial, Jesus did not conceal that he saw himself as 'the Son of the Blessed'. He even affirmed that one day they would see him sitting at the right hand of power and coming on the clouds of heaven. The high priest's response was entirely predictable: 'The high priest tore his clothes. "Why do we need any more witnesses?" he asked. "You have heard the blasphemy. What do you think?" They all condemned him as worthy of death' (Mark 14:63).

The truth is that, as portrayed in the Gospels (our only significant source of knowledge of Jesus), Jesus repeatedly speaks in a way that makes plain that he saw himself as divine. He allowed himself to be called 'Lord'. He referred to himself as the Son of God and to God as his Father (Abba). He claimed such divine prerogatives as forgiving sins. He allowed himself to be worshipped.

When Paul began to write his letters, not much more than ten years had passed since the death of Jesus. Many of those who had been closest to him were still alive and were themselves worshipping him: men like Peter, James and John in particular. The case of James is especially interesting. His letter may well be earlier than any of Paul's. He was Jesus' brother. He was highly respected by the Jews. Yet he unquestionably regarded Jesus as divine. He called him *Lord* (James 1:1) and even the *glory* (James 2:1) and spoke of himself not only as the servant/slave of God but as the servant/slave of Jesus Christ.

Besides all of which, there was the resurrection. If Christ had remained dead, it would have been impossible for Paul (or anyone else) to convince any Jew that he was divine. But the evidence that Jesus had risen was strong: and it was especially strong to the apostles, because they had seen him for themselves.

In fact we have to ask, how, apart from the resurrection of Christ, can we account for Paul's religion at all? Why did he come to worship Jesus in the first place, unless what he says happened on the Damascus Road actually did happen: that there he met the risen Christ? And if he has risen, then his claim to be divine is perfectly respectable and credible, in fact, inescapable.

We cannot use Paul to explain the rise of Christianity. We need Christianity to explain Paul.

Inconsistent with divine unity

The second Jewish objection to the divine sonship of Jesus is that it is inconsistent with the unity of God. If the doctrine of the Trinity is correct, there are three gods.

How can we then say, 'Hear, O Israel, the LORD our God, the LORD is *one*'.

Surely the answer to this is that we must take our idea of the unity of God from his Word, not from our own *a priori* notions. How can Jews account for some of the remarkable features of their own Scriptures: that the name for God is plural; that in Genesis 1:26, he says, 'Let *us*!'; and that in Isaiah 6:8 he says, 'Who will go for *us*?' Who was the Spirit of God? Who was the Angel of the Lord?

More fundamentally, there are very great difficulties in the idea of God existing for countless ages as a solitary being. Could such a being be self-conscious? Could he be a person (when he had nothing to relate to)? Could he be blessed (happy)? Could he be love, when he had none to love? Why, when he came to make men in his image, did he make him for fellowship if he himself knew no fellowship? Furthermore, is such a being the highest that can be conceived? Surely not. The mind cannot conceive a greater mystery than the three in one; or a higher form of existence than that of an intense fellowship of love; or a more glorious explanation of the divine independence than Father, Son and Spirit living eternally towards one another. Once we have seen that, 'less would not satisfy and more is not desired'. We take our choice: this doctrine is either too good to be true or good enough to be true.

The Messiah is not divine

Thirdly, Jews object that the expected Messiah was not a divine being or even a supernatural one. He would not have the right to forgive sin. Far less would he be confused with God. To quote Rabbi Isidore Epstein again: 'At the highest the Messiah is but a mortal leader who will be instrumental in fully rehabilitating Israel in its ancient homeland, and through a restored Israel bring about the moral and spiritual regeneration of the whole of humanity, making all mankind fit citizens of the Kingdom' (*Judaism*, p. 140).

One drawback with this standard Jewish view of the Messiah is that he has not come: and fewer and fewer Jews seem to believe he will ever come. It looks very much as if to deny that Jesus is the Messiah is to give up hope of a Messiah altogether.

Another problem is that such a view of the Messiah is hardly a worthy one. It is nationalistic and materialistic. It does not deal with the deepest problem facing man: sin. It does not meet man's deepest fear: death. It does not match man's highest conceptions: the Messiah personally sharing our sorrow, bearing our sins, conquering death, procuring life and immortality and filling our hearts with the prospect of a new heaven and a new earth.

But surely the most important question is this: did Jewish expectation measure up to God's promise? Granted that they looked only for one to restore glory to Israel and put their enemies to shame, but is that what the Old Testament had led them to hope? Jesus certainly did not think so. He accused even his own disciples of being foolish and 'slow of heart to believe all that the prophets have spoken' (Luke 24:25). The stricture appears fully justified. The term *Messiah* first appears in Psalm 2:2; 'The rulers gather together against the Lord and against his *Anointed One.*' In this psalm the Messiah is clearly the Son of God, glorious enough to hold sway over the whole world and to be invincible and dreadful if provoked. All are commanded to swear allegiance to him, just as they are summoned to serve the Lord. 'Kiss the Son, lest he be angry and you be destroyed in your way' (Ps. 2:12). Other parts of the Old Testament speak in similar terms. According to Psalm 96:13 and Psalm 98:9 it is the Lord himself who is coming to vindicate his people.

Nothing short of a divine Messiah could do justice to such expectations. Certainly, once we have caught a glimpse (or even dreamt) of such a Saviour, nothing else can satisfy. We *need* to be able to say, as we respond to the blessings of our religion: 'No eye has seen, no ear has heard, no mind has conceived what God has prepared for those who love him' (1 Cor. 2:9).

A Christian can say that. But can a Jew? For him, God's provision is smaller even than our human hopes.

Islam

Mohammed, born in Mecca in 570 A.D., would have had contact with both Jews and Christians in his native city and also in Medina, to which he fled in 622 A.D. Unfortunately, the kind of Christianity he would have met would have been hopelessly corrupt and his own religion, in many of its features, was a reaction to it.

At one level, Mohammed had a high view of Jesus. He regarded him as a prophet (indeed one of the greatest of the prophets) and his followers as possessed, therefore, of authentic revelation. Christians, like the Jews, were 'people of the Book'. At one point in the Koran he writes: 'If the People of the Book believe and fear God, we shall expiate their sins and introduce them into gardens of delight: and if they observe the gospel and that which has been revealed to them from their Lord, they shall eat both from above and from under their feet. Among them is a righteous people, but evil is that which many of them do' (Fifth Sura). Another Sura gives a history of the early years of Christ, including accounts of the Annunciation and of the early years of John the Baptist. Broadly, Mohammed's view was that the Christian Scriptures represented truth for their own time, but they had been superseded by the revelation God had given to *him*.

Mohammed himself clearly misunderstood the doctrine of the Trinity. According to J. N. D. Anderson, 'There is no manner of doubt that he believed the Christian Trinity to consist of the Father, the Virgin and their Child' (*The World's Religions*, Inter-Varsity Press, 1963, p. 62). This can easily be confirmed from the Koran itself. To quote just one example: in Sura XIX.91 we read, 'They say: "The God of Mercy hath gotten offspring." Now have ye done a monstrous thing! Almost might the very heavens be rent thereat, and the

Earth cleave asunder, and the mountains fall down in fragments, that they ascribe a son to the God of Mercy, when it beseemeth not the God of Mercy to beget a son!' Within such a framework, the sonship of Jesus could be understood only physically. It was the result of sexual union between the Father and the Virgin Mary. Not surprisingly, Mohammed regarded this as blasphemous. On the other hand, objections against the Christian doctrine so understood are clearly aimed at a man of straw. Christians have never believed the ideas Mohammed attributes to them here.

According to the Koran, Jesus never claimed deity. Unfortunately the Koran also denies that he died on the cross. Instead, when the Jews tried to crucify him, God caught him up to heaven and someone else was crucified in his place. The one statement is no more worthy of belief than the other. The New Testament makes plain that the notion of the deity of Christ was not something that dawned gradually on the church. It was there from the beginning; or at least from very soon after the resurrection. As we have seen, there was no argument or debate about it. The position reflected in the earliest letters (Galatians, James, 1 Thessalonians) was accepted without controversy. According to the Gospels, this attitude to Jesus on the part of the disciples went right back to his attitude to himself. Indeed, it is impossible to understand how it could have arisen in any other way. Those who came to worship Jesus as the Son of God were monotheists of the deepest dye. The idea of deifying a man would have been abhorrent to James (and to Peter, Paul and John).

On the other hand, if Jesus did in fact claim to be God, Muslims will have to revise their whole opinion of him. They will either have to accept his claim or reject it. If they accept it, they must go on to worship him. If they reject it, they must repudiate him unreservedly. A man who calls himself *God* cannot be a prophet. He is either a knave or a fool and his proper place is either on a gallows (which is what the Jews thought) or in an institution (the normal place for those who think they are either God or Napoleon).

The real reason for Mohammed's aversion to the doctrine of the Trinity probably had little to do with history. It was a matter of theological first principles: nothing could be allowed to threaten the unity and transcendence of God. How could the high and holy One become flesh? (Peter expressed essentially the same objection when he said, 'You shall never wash my feet!' John 13:8.) And how could the one God have a Son and a Spirit sharing fully in his nature and in his authority? After all, Islam began with Mohammed's daring condemnation of the idolatry of Mecca: he was hardly going to endorse what he saw as the three gods of Christianity.

What can a Christian say? Only, once more, that the idea of God as an Eternal Solitary is both exceedingly difficult and exceedingly unsatisfactory. That God is one is not in doubt. What is in doubt is the nature of this oneness. According to Christianity it is the oneness of an eternal fellowship of love in which the Father, the Son and the Holy Spirit share the one being and exercise the one authority, and yet relate to one another in all the warmth and withness of a personal relationship. What is at stake is whether God is personal or abstract: and once we have caught a glimpse of the former we can never return to the latter.

8

Mormonism and Jehovah's Witnesses

Mormonism

Mormons profess to take their doctrine from the Bible. Indeed, one of their recent publications even goes so far as to say, 'Bible doctrine is Mormon doctrine and Mormon doctrine is Bible doctrine' (*What the Mormons Think of Christ*, 1982, p.3). Unfortunately, the position is not that simple. Mormons also claim to possess 'latter day revelation', consisting mainly of the *Book of Mormon* but supplemented by even later revelations contained in *Doctrine and Covenants*, *Pearl of Great Price* and the pronouncements of their Presidents and other officials. All this makes life very difficult for anyone who wants to know exactly what Mormons teach. Many of the statements contained in these documents are unintelligible. Many more are mutually inconsistent: what is said in one place is taken back in another and the student is conscious of being very vulnerable. Mormons can always quote from their sacred books some statement or other which suggests that they do not hold the doctrines attributed to them.

One thing can be said with confidence, however: Mormons believe that Jesus Christ is the Son of God. The Lamb of God is the Son of the Eternal Father and the Saviour of the world, we read in 1 Nephi 13:40. He is also called explicitly the Only Begotten: Isaac was 'a similitude of God and his Only Begotten Son' (Jacob 4:50). But this turns out to mean something quite different from what it has meant in Christianity.

First, the *Book of Mormon* also appears to regard Jesus as *the Father*. For example, in Mosiah 16:15 we read, 'Look then what redemption cometh through Christ the Lord, who is *the very Eternal Father*'. The identification is even more explicit in Mormon 9:12: 'And because of the fall of man came Jesus Christ, even the Father and the Son'. If these statements are to be taken literally Mormons see no distinction between the Father and the Son: which is as much as to say that neither the Father nor the Son really exists. They are only different names for the same 'person'.

Secondly, however, Mormons seem to teach the opposite: something very like polytheism (a plurality of gods). It is difficult to understand how this came about, since the *Book of Mormon* itself stresses the unity of God.

In 2 Nephi 31:21, for example, we read: 'And now, behold, this is the doctrine of Christ, and the only true doctrine of the Father, and of the Son and of the Holy Ghost, which is one God, without end'. As early as 1844, however, Joseph Smith (supposed to be an errorless prophet) was teaching something completely different: 'I will preach on the plurality of gods. I have always declared God to be a distinct personage. Jesus Christ a separate and distinct personage from God the Father, and that the Holy Ghost was a distinct personage and a Spirit: and these three constitute three distinct personages and three gods'.

In fact, Smith cannot conceal his contempt for the doctrine of the Trinity: 'Many even say there is one God; the Father, the Son and the Holy Ghost are only one God. I say that is a strange God anyhow – three in one, and one in three! It is a curious organisation.... All are to be crammed into one God, according to the sectarianism (sic). It would make the biggest God in all the world. He would be a wonderfully big God – he would be a giant or a monster' (Sermon on The Christian Godhead – Plurality of Gods, quoted in A. A. Hoekema, *The Four Major Cults*, 1969, p.35).

Apart from all else, this raises a huge problem of consistency. Joseph Smith and 2 Nephi 31:21 cannot both be correct. In fact Smith appears to have held that the world was created not by God but by the gods, and although there is only one god for *us* (or for this earth), other things and other planets have other gods. The one argument produced in support of this is that throughout the Old Testament (and particularly in Gen. 1:26) the word for God is the plural *Elohim*. But the author of Genesis never expected the divine name to be understood as referring to more than one God. It is always used with singular verbs, singular adjectives and singular pronouns.

Thirdly, Mormons have a startling view of the actual nature of the sonship of Jesus. They regard him as *physically* the Son of God. The document *What the Mormons Think of Christ* makes this plain: when it asks, rhetorically, 'Is he really the Son of God, as we are the sons of mortal fathers? Or was he the greatest moral and spiritual teacher of all ages, though not the literal, personal offspring in the flesh of that exalted, personal being who is God our Father?' (page 6). The idea suggested here is stated more firmly on the following page. 'Many reliable surveys have been made among present-day ministers and lay-men, inquiring relative to a belief in Christ as the literal Son of God. Few have knowledge that he is such, literally, personally, actually, as other men are the sons of mortal parents.' Underlying this particular doctrine is a rejection of the spirituality of God: 'When one believes God to be impersonal, uncreated, incorporeal... a mystical three-in-one spirit that fills immensity, it is not possible to accept him as the literal Father of our Lord.'

In the *Book of Mormon* such notions are only vaguely hinted at. In 1 Nephi 11:18, for example, we read, 'Behold the virgin whom thou seest is the mother of the Son of God, *after the manner of the flesh*' (italics mine). There is a more obscure passage to similar effect in Mosiah 15

(vv. 2ff.): 'And because he dwelleth in the flesh he shall be called the Son of God, and having subjected the flesh to the will of the Father, being the Father and the Son – the Father, because he was conceived by the power of God; and the Son, because of the flesh.'

In later Mormon pronouncement the idea of the literal, physical sonship of Christ is explicit. President Brigham Young once declared that the body of Christ was begotten (of the Virgin) by Adam, 'after the same manner as the tabernacles (that is, the bodies) of Cain, Abel and the rest of the sons and daughters of Adam and Eve.' Joseph Fielding Smith and James E Talmage attempted to deliver Mormonism from this embarrassment, but succeeded only in making matters worse. According to the former, 'Our Father in heaven is the Father of Jesus Christ, both in the spirit and in the flesh.' According to the latter, Christ is 'the offspring of a mortal mother and of an immortal, or resurrected and glorified, Father.' What can this mean but that Jesus Christ was the product of a physical union between God the Father and Mary? As we have seen, Mormonism denies the spirituality of God. The Father as well as the Son has a body of flesh and bones, as tangible as man's. In fact, to Mormonism *personal* seems to mean *physical*. Against such a background all that God does, including begetting, has physical overtones.

Finally, according to Mormon theology Christ is no more divine than the rest of us. At one end of the story 'all men lived in a premortal state before they were born'. They were 'spirit children of the Father'. The only distinction of Christ is that he was the firstborn spirit child. *Doctrine and Covenants* (93:21-23) represents him as saying, 'Ye were also in the beginning with the Father.' From this point of view, Christ is slightly older, but no greater.

At the other end of the story, Mormonism suggests that men may become gods. The idea does not occur in the *Book of Mormon* but it was certainly preached unambiguously by Joseph Smith: 'Here, then, is eternal life – to know the only wise and true God; and you have got to learn how to be gods yourselves and to be kings and priests to God, the same as all gods have done before you, namely, by going from one small degree to another, and from a small capacity to a great one.' In fact, as the closing words of this quotation suggest, all the gods were once men. The idea is asserted unashamedly: according to Smith himself, 'God himself was once as we are now, and is exalted man'; and a more recent President, Lorenzo Snow, tells us, 'As man is, God once was: as God is, man may become.'

Such ideas hardly need refutation. Mormonism requires total intellectual abdication: faith in plates which no man has seen; submission to a translation we are in no position to verify; and a return to the basest elements of pagan mythology. The loyalty which the system commands is undeniable. But it wasn't built on argument: and it can't be refuted by it.

Jehovah's Witnesses

Unlike the Mormons, Jehovah's Witnesses do not have any authoritative books apart from the Bible. In practice, unfortunately, the Bible is subjected to traditional Watchtower theology. But it still remains true that if we want to know what Jehovah's Witnesses believe, the best place to go is their official version of the Scriptures, *The New World Translation* (Revised Edition, 1984, published by the Watchtower Bible and Tract Society of New York).

Jehovah

The first thing to strike the reader of this version is the frequency with which the name *Jehovah* occurs. Witnesses regard this as the only true name of God and in the Old Testament section of the translation it is used consistently to render the sacred designation, JHWH. It is also used in the New Testament, however: 237 times in the text of the translation and over 70 times in the footnotes. There is absolutely no warrant for this.

In the original, the name *Jehovah* never occurs. In the *New World Translation* it is occasionally offered as a rendering of *theos* (God) and frequently as a rendering of *kurios* (Lord). There is some justification for the latter: in the Greek translation of the Old Testament (known as the Septuagint) *kurios* was the usual translation of JHWH.

But Jehovah's Witnesses do not carry this through consistently. At points which are crucially important theologically, they do not translate *kurios* by *Jehovah*. The most notable example is Philippians 2:11, 'Jesus Christ is Lord!' Here, if anywhere in the New Testament, there is a case for translating *kurios* by *Jehovah*. We have been told in verse 9 that the name given to Jesus is 'the name above every name'; and the words in verse 10 are a quotation from Isaiah 45:23, referring specifically to Jehovah: 'to me every knee will bend down, every tongue will swear'. If the *New World Translation* were consistent, it would render Philippians 2:11, 'Jesus Christ is Jehovah'.

Christ

This would be too high a price to pay for consistency, however. Jehovah's Witnesses deny the deity of Christ and in the *New World Translation* this doctrine is eliminated from most (but not all) of the passages which seem to teach it. The most notorious example is John 1:1: 'the Word was a god' (we have already discussed this translation on pages 22-24). In John 1:18, *theos* is again translated without a capital when it refers to Jesus: 'No man has seen God at any time; the only begotten god who is in the bosom of the Father is the one that has explained him.' The same approach is taken in John 10:33: 'The Jews answered him: "We are stoning you, not for a fine work, but for blasphemy, even because you, although being a man, make yourself a god."' Apart altogether from grammatical considerations, this is rank polytheism: and we cannot get over the difficulty by having a graduated scale of deities, culminating in one with a capital G.

The *New World Translation* also departs from the rules of grammar in translating such passages as Titus 2:13. The fact that the two phrases, *the great God* and *our Saviour Jesus Christ* are covered by the one definite article strongly suggests that they refer to the one person: 'our great God and Saviour, Jesus Christ.' But the *New World Translation* distinguishes them sharply (and inelegantly!): 'We wait for the happy hope and glorious manifestation of the great God and of (the) Savior of us, Christ Jesus.' The same thing is done with 2 Peter 1:1, a passage with a similar construction. The *New World Translation* renders it 'by the righteousness of our God and [the] Savior Jesus Christ.' The definite article in brackets has no justification whatever in the text.

Such renderings have nothing at all to do with objective scholarship. They are unsophisticated reflections of theological bias. Jehovah's Witnesses are Unitarians: in fact, to be more precise, they are latter-day Arians. An official statement of their beliefs appears regularly on the first page of their magazine, *The Watchtower*, and in it they declare that 'Jehovah is the only true God and is the Maker of heaven and earth and the Giver of life to his creatures'. Christ, the Logos, is sharply distinguished from Jehovah. He is a creature: 'the Logos was the beginning of his creation'. He was the spokesman of God. He was the Chief Executive Officer of Jehovah. He was the archangel Michael. He was a god. But he was not eternal. He is not immortal. And he is not God.

The Holy Spirit

If Jehovah's Witnesses have a low view of Christ they have an even lower view of the Holy Spirit. They deny both his deity and his personality and regard him as only the 'invisible, active force of God'. This disparagement is seen in the very typography of the *New World Translation*. It capitalises words which refer to God and words which refer to Christ. But it never capitalises the word *spirit*, even when it occurs in the combination *the holy spirit*. For example, it translates Matthew 28:19 as follows: 'Go therefore and make disciples of people of all the nations, baptising them in the name of the Father and of the Son and of the holy spirit.' We find the same thing in 2 Corinthians 13:14: 'The undeserved kindness of the Lord Jesus Christ and the love of God and the sharing in the holy spirit be with all of YOU' (the YOU in block capitals is to indicate a plural).

Deity of the Spirit

The evidence for the deity of the Holy Spirit is not as full as for the deity of Christ, largely because the Spirit's work is to draw attention to the Saviour, not to himself: 'he will bring glory to me by taking from what is mine and making it known to you' (John 16:14). Yet we are left in no doubt as to his divine nature and his right, with the Father and the Son, to be worshipped and glorified.

Firstly, the name of God is applied to him, not directly but by implication. We see this very clearly in Acts 5:3-4.

In verse 3, Peter charges Ananias with lying to the *Holy Spirit*. In verse 4 he charges him with lying to *God*. To do the one implied the other. This is clear even from the *New World Translation* itself: 'You have played false, not to men, but to God.' The same conclusion can be drawn from 1 Corinthians 3:16. To be indwelt by the Spirit means to be indwelt by God: 'Don't you know that you yourselves are God's temple and that God's Spirit lives in you?' And, with or without capitals, the holy spirit of Matthew 28:19 shares equally with the Father and the Son in the one divine name.

Secondly, the apostles regarded the Holy Spirit as being, as much as the Father and the Son, the source of the blessings of redemption. This appears most clearly in 2 Corinthians 13:14: 'May the grace of the Lord Jesus Christ, and the love of God, and the fellowship of the Holy Spirit be with you all'. It is implied, too, in the greeting of Revelation 1:4: 'Grace and peace to you from him who is, and who was, and who is to come, and from the seven spirits before his throne, and from Jesus Christ.' The phrase *the seven spirits* probably means the seven-fold Spirit or the Holy Ghost in his fulness and completeness (seven being the symbol of perfection). The words of the Great Commission surely point in the same direction. We are baptized into the threefold name because we belong to the Three: and we belong because our redemption has been the work not of the Father alone, or of the Father and the Son together, but of the Father, the Son and the Holy Spirit.

Thirdly, and perhaps most interesting of all, there is the Lord's reference in Luke 12:8-10 to the gravity of speaking evil of the Holy Spirit: 'Everyone that says a word against the Son of Man, it will be forgiven him; but he that blasphemes against the holy spirit will not be forgiven it' (*New World Translation*). This does not mean that the Spirit is greater than Christ. But the glory of Christ is veiled in the incarnation, especially during his ministry on earth; ignorance of his deity is excusable. But the unforgivableness of blaspheming the Holy Spirit surely proves that his glory is fully equal to that of the Father and the Son.

The Spirit's personality

The *New World Translation* also betrays at once its attitude to the *personality* of the Holy Spirit: it refers to him repeatedly as *it* and *which*. John 14:26, for example, reads: 'the helper, the holy spirit, *which* the Father will send in my name'. Romans 8:16 is rendered, 'The spirit *itself* bears witness with our spirit'. A similar approach is taken to Ephesians 4:30: 'Do not be grieving God's holy spirit, with *which* you have been sealed'.

The only remotely plausible argument for this is that in Greek *spirit* (*pneuma*) is neuter and therefore pronouns referring to him are neuter, too. But Greek, like many other languages, has grammatical, not natural, gender. Masculines do not refer only to men or feminines only to women or neuters only to things. *Day*, for example, is feminine, but that does not lead the *New World*

Translation to refer to it as *she*. *Child*, like *spirit*, is neuter. Do we therefore regard children as things?

As if this were not enough, in the New Testament itself the masculine personal pronoun (*ekeinos*) is applied to the Spirit repeatedly, (just as *elohim*, the plural name for God, always has a singular verb). We see this, for example, in John 16:8 ('*he* will convict the world of guilt') and in John 16:14 ('*he* will bring glory to me'). In such passages the sense of the personality of the Spirit is so strong as to override considerations of grammar.

But this is only one item in an overwhelming body of New Testament evidence that the Holy Spirit is a person, and not just an abstract force or influence. We must limit ourselves to three points.

First, there is the work the Spirit does. He is the Counsellor (the Paraclete): not the divine comfort, but the divine comfort*er*, able to take Christ's place when he goes (John 14:16, 18). He convicts of guilt (John 16:8). He witnesses to Christ, just as the apostles do (John 15:26-27). He leads us, witnesses to us and helps us (Rom. 8:14, 16, 26). He even intercedes for us with 'groans that words cannot express' (Rom. 8:26).

Secondly, there is the role of the Spirit in the life of the early church. It is the Spirit who sends men out to new work: 'The Holy Spirit said, "Set apart for me Barnabas and Saul for the work to which I have called them"' (Acts 13:2). Later, the same Spirit prevents them from entering into certain areas: 'having been kept by the Holy Spirit from preaching the word in the province of Asia' (Acts 16:6). In

Acts 20:28 it is the Spirit who makes men overseers of the church; and according to Acts 20:23 it was the Holy Spirit who, through the prophets, was warning Paul that 'prison and hardship' was facing him. No abstract force could be spoken of in such terms.

Finally, there is the Spirit's reaction to human behaviour. The language used by the Bible in this connection makes no sense unless it applies to a person. For example, in Acts 5:3 Ananias is accused of *lying* to the Spirit. You cannot lie to 'an invisible, active force'. Nor can you *tempt* it, as Sapphira is said to have done (Acts 5:9). Even less can you speak of it as Isaiah does (63:10): 'Yet they rebelled and grieved his Holy Spirit. So he turned and became their enemy and he himself fought against them'. This is the background to Paul's words in Ephesians 4:30: 'Do not grieve the Holy Spirit of God, with whom you were sealed for the day of redemption'.

As H. C. G. Moule pointed out many years ago, 'Only a Person can be *put to pain* by moral wrong'. In fact there is an interesting commentary on this verse in the *Shepherd of Hermas* (written before the middle of the second century): 'Put away therefore from thyself sadness, and afflict not the Holy Spirit that dwelleth in thee, lest haply he intercede with God against thee, and depart from thee' (M. 10.ii).

Conclusion

The doctrine of the Trinity has obviously not had an easy time in the world. Today, as ever, it attracts the antagonism of those who prefer unambiguous simplicity. But the objections have changed little over the centuries. And while we may feel uneasy with some of the terminology, we have yet to find better words to express the truth.

'This is the Catholic Faith: That we worship one
    God in Trinity, and Trinity in Unity;
Neither confounding the Persons: nor
    dividing the Essence.
For there is one Person of the Father: and another of
    the Son: and another of the Holy Spirit.
But the Godhead of the Father, of the Son, and of
    the Holy Spirit, is all one: the Glory equal, the
    Majesty coeternal.'

The Athanasian Creed

Scripture Index

General Index